Note to Self

A Music Director's Guide for Transitioning to a New School and Building a Thriving Music Program

Adrian Gordon

Leap Year Music Publishing
An Exclusive Music Collection

Contact information for Leap Year Music Publishing– www.leapyearmusic.com

ISBN: 979-8-218-04184-7 (paperback)
ISBN: 979-8-9866499-0-0 (ebook)

Ordering Information:
Special discounts are available on quantity purchases by corporations, associations, and others. For details, contact: adrian@adriangordonmusic.com

Dedication

*To my fellow music educators, who tirelessly strive to leave
our profession in better shape than they found it.*

Table of Contents

Introduction

Y ou got the music director gig—congratulations! You are about to step into a great new working environment that promises to be a step up from what you were doing before. But now what?

In college, we learned several semesters' worth of content on how to be effective musicians and educators, but nobody taught us how we can best manage changing environments and expectations for ourselves—and for our students—when we transition between jobs. Often, we work so hard to attain the position we really want that we don't stop to think about what the transition into that new job will actually entail. Typically, the best practices regarding personal health, job transitions, and change management are not explicitly discussed in our music school training. So, how do we make our transitions between schools as seamless and successful as possible while preserving our physical, mental, and emotional health? What do we need to take into consideration?

Navigating the scope of a new music director job can be particularly difficult if you are transitioning into an already-established music program with its own entrenched culture and traditions. This book can help you! The idea behind *Note to Self* is to help music teachers develop the tools necessary to transition into their new jobs as smoothly and healthfully as possible. This book is written for the hard-working teacher who needs straightforward, practical tips and ideas to help navigate the transition into their new school music job. No fluff or academic jargon—just chapter after chapter of practical tips and ideas to consider as you move into your new role.

I have personally been through four transitions in two different schools: general music, choir, and two string orchestra positions. While my undergraduate (BA music) and graduate (MS music education) programs were musically and pedagogically extensive, they never really touched on those hard-to-navigate areas of transitioning between jobs.

In this book, you will discover the tools for managing change and expectations when transitioning into a new music director position. Whether you are a new teacher or a veteran teacher transitioning into a new position, there is something here for you! I wish I would have had someone to tell me what to expect and what to consider in the transitions throughout my own career.

Thankfully, I have seen each and every one of my programs over the past 17 years grow in numbers and quality. In this book, I'll share what I've learned, along with the mistakes I made along the way. My hope is that you can avoid making the same mistakes I did.

In the chapters ahead, you'll learn tips on self-care, what to prepare during your summer, how to gain the trust of your community, what to expect in the first few years, and how to keep your program growing. The tips in this book will allow you to be proactive and prepared when you arrive at your new role and greet your new students.

At the beginning of each chapter, you'll find a song title that reflects the spirit of each chapter and is a fun way to help you musically flesh out the content as you read. There are also thoughtful reflection questions at the end of each section to help you clarify your purpose, goals, and strategies. Apply the strategies in this book, and you'll be able to build the best working and learning environment you've ever been a part of, for you and your students!

CHAPTER 1

"Human Nature" by Michael Jackson

Why vs. What

The inherent social component within our programs high-lights how important it is for music educators to remember that we are not solely in the field of music but also in the field of *people*. That social component is often overlooked.

A key element of building a strong, cohesive program is showing your students that your "*why*" (your passion to invest in their development as people) is informing your "*what*" (teaching them about music). As music educators, we should be introspective and keenly aware of our reasons for what we are doing.

In the midst of a positive and exciting job change, we can easily lose sight of the bigger picture: our professional purpose. There are lesson plans to create, pieces of sheet music to purchase, people to meet, instruments to clean; the list goes on and on. In the thick of it all, reflecting on our personal answers to the very important question of why we endeavor to teach music to kids can help us find our direction, focus, and purpose while transitioning into a new position, even while everything around us changes at lightning speed.

Many educators would agree that, while teaching is a noble profession, it definitely isn't a profession that one enters because of the high salary and lavish lifestyle. For teachers, the reward is less about monetary value and more about the long-term success of the people we have invested in. We love our craft—music—but, more importantly, we share a deep sense of care for people. Music just happens to be the vehicle with which we show our students how much we care. This is personally true for me as well. My own "why" comes into focus when I get to see the light bulb in a student's mind go off. There is a certain joy in watching a student come to the realization that they are good at something and very capable of making great achievements. For me personally, this is what makes teaching worth it!

Some of the best teachers that I had in my own secondary education understood that, even if students didn't share their same passion for their discipline, in many ways their subjects were vehicles for helping to educate students beyond facts and figures. Teaching their disciplines was also a way to help raise a generation of thoughtful, critically thinking young people. There was a part of those teachers that saw past their subjects and was able to connect to their students on a human level. This approach made me much more willing to listen and follow those teachers' directives. Even if they were teaching subjects I disliked, I still knew that they cared!

As simple and cliché as it sounds, students will be much more receptive to your educational goals for the class if they know that they are seen and valued as people first. I have found this to be true in my own experience, especially in transitions where I was following beloved teachers who were leaving after several years. Though the trust that developed between me and my new students was not built overnight, showing them that I cared was a significant part of winning them over. It is a constant effort (and probably always will be) to show our students that we genuinely care for them.

In many ways, the job of a music educator encompasses more

than that of a normal academic teacher. The ensemble experience includes elements of a traditional curricular approach, as well as extracurricular elements similar to what you would see on an athletic team. Students have to intellectually absorb and perform the music material, yet their development, output, and success as an ensemble are contingent upon each member's accountability (academically and socially) to one another. Both elements are necessary to create a harmonious (pun intended) working environment that lends itself to a healthy and productive music-making experience.

Because our positions as music educators allow us to see our students grow and develop over several years, we have a unique opportunity that other academic teachers don't usually have to be consistent, positive forces in their lives. We get to be mentors who students will always remember fondly. A lot of the efforts to convey your care for your students or your "why" do not have to be overly complicated. They simply need to be sincere and consistent.

Whether you're transitioning into your new position, or you've been in the same role for a while, your students should know that you can look past the content of the class and see them as valuable individuals. While the goal of developing a high-performance level music program is admirable, it should be the by-product of a family-like atmosphere that promotes the care of the individual students as people instead of only as players in your ensembles. Don't let what you are teaching overshadow why you are teaching it.

What You Do

Now that you've reflected on your "why," it's time to translate your purpose into action. Our mission is to push our students toward excellence and help them reach their personal best, all the while showing them that we care.

Back when I was younger and performing with a band, I attended a clinic about songwriting and performing. The keynote speaker was a moderately successful band leader, singer, and song-writer. There was something that he said, very plainly and bluntly, that has stuck with me to this day. "Rule number one for being an artist in the music industry is 'Don't suck.' "

Now, that may seem very crass, but it nonetheless highlights an unavoidable truth for us as musicians and music educators. As cynical as it sounds, we can almost expect for people to not under-stand our profession and think that the work we are invested in is easy and doesn't require much expertise. Almost no one outside of our field will understand the skill development and the emotional and physical investments that we have to make behind the scenes to push our students and our programs to their greatest potential. We are the most successful in the classroom when we are consis-tently striving for our personal best as it pertains to our profession-alism and level of teaching in the classroom. This doesn't mean that you need to be a world-class musician who has come down from the heavens to grace your students. It simply means that you emulate an authentic level of passion and respect for your craft.

We tend to forget how much our students pick up from us when we are *not* intentionally teaching. At the beginning of my second year at my new school, I was asked to do an unusual wed-ding gig. The groom wanted a small orchestra to perform '90s booty-shaking music during the reception. I've played the violin at many wedding gigs before, but I had never been asked for such an unusual music request. Needless to say, I spent several hours prac-ticing on my violin the week before the wedding. One afternoon, I was practicing after school, and one of my students walked into the room. She was absolutely fascinated by the fact that her teacher was taking the time to practice his instrument. Her words were, "It's one thing for you to tell us to practice, but seeing *you* practice makes me think practicing is so much more important."

(The wedding gig went off without a hitch, and the bride and groom were very happy. Who would have thought "Tootsee Roll" by 69 Boyz performed by a string orchestra would have been a crowd favorite?)

Remember, students are watching what we do even when we're not trying to intentionally teach them something. Be aware of your influence. But, more than that, be open about striving for excellence in your own walk as a musician and music educator. Have fun! And, most importantly, don't suck!

1.   **What are you currently doing to communicate care (your "why") beyond academic achievement?**

---

2.   **What ideas can you add to your program that demonstrate care (your "why")?**

---

3.   **As you start off in a new position, where do you think you have room for improvement as an educator? What steps can you take to get better?**

CHAPTER 2

"There Will Never Be Another You" by
Harry Warren and Mack Gordon

Just Be Yourself

With only a few exceptions, my middle school and high school students were very untrusting of my motives, no matter how altruistic those motives were. Coming into my new position as music director at a new school, I felt like an outsider. I remember receiving AirDropped (immediate digital data transfers from device to device) pictures of the former director while I was on campus. There were no names attached identifying the senders, so it was impossible to figure out where the pictures were coming from. I figured they were coming from disgruntled students who wanted to voice their disapproval of my presence.

Clearly, I needed to do something to connect to my new community. I started to talk more about my journey as a musician, my role as a family man, and my goals as a teacher. Each discussion softened my students' hearts toward me and helped them see me as more human.

Having these discussions with the students made me reflect

7

on my character and ask myself a very poignant question: "Who am I?" The words that I chose as I entered my new position were *strong*, *gracious*, and *caring*. That was who I was. These were the character traits that I committed to sharing with my new community. This meant that when students around campus sent anonymous digital jabs to my phone, I didn't let their behavior deter me from my objective of helping them in their music education. I would tell them, "While I am not your former director, I am here to help you in any way that I can."

When students would complain about certain performance assessment grades, I gave them the opportunity to retake those assessments as many times as it took for them to get it right and improve their grades. This also meant that I would plan fun after-school events like movie nights to build community and to show them that I cared for them as people. Showing the students who I was, instead of only telling them who I was, ended up being a vital part of not only building a relationship with my new students but also establishing my identity within the school.

As you enter your new role, consider writing down three to five positive words that describe who you are as a person. Think carefully about those words. Once you have put them on paper, save them. Return to them often, especially when you need to reflect on who you are as an educator, even in the most difficult times.

Because we typically expect to have longevity in our new positions, it is important that we reflect on who we are and what we will be projecting during our first encounters with our new community. This is especially true as music educators, because in many cases, the enlistment by students into our programs, unlike other academic classes, is optional. It is in your best interest to set an authentic, positive tone for the year, which will help you create an environment where longevity is possible. The process of self-reflecting on your character and also living out those positive qualities that you have listed will help create that environment.

Filter your day-to-day interactions through the lens of those descriptors. It will be important to use these words as a character guide as you have day-to-day interactions with your new community. Your character may be questioned by students, parents, and colleagues who do not know you. Put your best foot forward as much as possible. Make sure that every interaction with your new community reflects the words that you wrote down, especially in your first-time interactions. Remember that these words, no matter how true they are to you, are unknown to your new community with respect to your character.

One way to internalize your words is by reciting them each morning before you get out of your car. You can even make it community-based by writing your descriptors on your board with the heading "I choose to be ..." Ask the students to think through their own descriptors and share them so that everyone becomes invested in keeping each other accountable. The most important points to remember are that, regardless of how you decide to internalize the descriptors that you picked, they should be true to who you are and that you should act accordingly. No more, no less.

Impostor Syndrome

*Bonus Track: "I Have Confidence" from *The Sound of Music*

The discomfort of a new environment, along with the necessary social and professional adjustment period, can sometimes cause a feeling of impostor syndrome. Impostor syndrome is a feeling of inadequacy, sometimes coupled with the feeling that discovery by others of your inadequacy is imminent in a particular area (despite having real and tangible prior markers of success).[1]

---

[1] "Imposter Syndrome," *Psychology Today*, accessed April 3, 2022, https://www.psychologytoday.com/us/basics/imposter-syndrome.

I remember how, when I made the transition from just teaching elementary and middle school orchestra to teaching elementary, middle, and now high school concurrently, I felt as though impostor syndrome was creeping into my psyche. Although I had taught high school–level repertoire at the middle school level, I had never taught high school students. For all the worrying I did, once I got started with our daily rehearsals and interactions, it was a very joyful experience. I ended up getting along very well with the high school students. All the worrying I had done had been in vain. Looking back on that experience, I wish I would have trusted in my prior markers of success. I had been successful in teaching every level up to that point, and there was nothing to indicate that I would have performed any differently with high school students—nothing except my own insecurity stemming from impostor syndrome.

Impostor syndrome can derail your efforts to confidently establish yourself in your new role. Don't let your new environment throw you off your game. Your accomplishments and the path that led you to your current position are real and impressive in their own right. You couldn't have gotten the job in the first place if this wasn't true.

As you begin shaping or reshaping your program, you will start to find that some people will appreciate what you are doing and that some people won't. Like anything else in life, you can't make everybody happy. As a matter of fact, the longer I am a teacher, the more I realize that some people aren't happy unless they are unhappy, and those unhappy folks tend to have a way of turning our worlds upside down. It can be very easy to let negative comments and experiences hijack your days, weeks, or months.

Writing the positive exchanges down on paper can help drown out the negative noise and remind you of the good you are doing in the lives of the students around you. Let the positive vibes recharge you. You will never have a shortage of complaints and grievances, so always try, even if only for a moment, to appreciate the positive feedback from students, parents, and colleagues. Remember that you were hired for a reason. You have a particular skill set that is valuable to many.

Being Professional in the Face of Adversity

Just as in every other aspect of life, you will most likely face obstacles to your professional goals and vision when you transition into a new role. We may sometimes see obstacles put before us by our own community of colleagues, administrators, parents, students, or all of the above. Remember, the fact that others may try to undermine elements of your goals and vision does not take away the merit and validity of those goals and that vision.

Many times, administrators and school boards make decisions that don't necessarily take workplace morale or teachers' well-being into account and are counterproductive to developing a strong music program. You might vehemently disagree with decisions being made around you—they may very well be pedagogically egregious! But think about the big picture, which ultimately is your well-being. Remember that it is not the decisions made beyond your control that define you. You are defined by the way you choose to respond.

Try not to let the obstacles discourage you. The stress is not worth carrying. There is no award for being the most stressed-out teacher. Continue to strive for excellence within your reach. Choose to stay positive. Acknowledge the challenges before you and move forward without carrying the weight of the world on your shoulders. Be strong, be kind, be bold, be smart, be creative, but most importantly, be professional!

Comparisons

As you settle into your new position, be prepared to receive both positive and negative comparisons between you and your predecessor. Students, parents, and administrators will unintentionally make comparisons to help them make sense of the current climate compared to what they already knew. As unfair as it may seem, this is bound to happen.

Some of the comments may be shared with you directly, and some comments may come to you through the grapevine. One can hope that the majority of feedback in those early days is positive.

Whatever the comments may be, and however they reach you, be sure to remain professional in every situation. Be humbled by the nice things, be open minded to the negative comments that may reach you, and in both cases, see if there is any sliver of truth in the comments you hear that may allow you to reevaluate your own actions and methodologies so that you may grow. Never apologize for being yourself—only for not striving to be the best version of yourself.

In Case You Forget

*Bonus Track: "Because You Loved Me" by Céline Dion

Everyone needs an emotional pick-me-up from time to time. Kind words of affirmation can lift your spirits and point you back in the right direction when you are faced with difficult situations in your new position. Hold on to letters, cards, and emails from former students that speak to your positive influence in their lives. If your transition happens to feel particularly harsh, look back on those messages. Let them bolster you and remind you of the great impact that you have had in the lives of other students. You have a lot to offer, and *there will never be another you.*

1. **What 3–5 positive words would describe you as a person?**

_____

2. What are you most confident in with regard to your teaching skills?

   _____

3. In what ways will those 3–5 words be visible to your new community?

   _____

4. What is the nicest thing a student or parent has ever said or written to you?

   _____

CHAPTER 3

"Signed, Sealed, Delivered (I'm Yours)" by Stevie Wonder

Now That It's Official

So, the job is yours! You're psyched and high on adrenaline. But what do you do now?

While the possibilities are endless, every journey needs a starting point. Getting yourself ready mentally and professionally can go a long way in creating a smooth transition.

Going into the summer after my last year at my old position, everything felt the same as it always had. It felt like any other summer that I had grown accustomed to enjoying. Looking back on that time, it was almost like the calm before the storm. It wasn't until a week or two before my designated time to report to my new job that I felt a slight sense of panic, intrigue, joy, and hope, all at the same time.

In retrospect, I had a false sense of security about my new position because of all the experiences I had gained in my old positions. While many skill sets and experiences carried over (conducting, performing, addressing technical issues, and employing interpersonal skills), in retrospect, there were other areas of preparation that were school specific and needed a more proactive approach. These are some ideas that may help you on your journey to thrive and become better acclimated in your new environment.

Meet and Greet

A valuable experience that I had before entering my new position was setting up a time with the outgoing director to meet my future students. This was an important factor in helping to maintain stability in the program for the upcoming school year. Being able to talk with me, ask questions, and play music together was a valuable experience for my future students as they were making up their minds as to whether they wanted to continue in the music program with me as their leader.

If you have any fun and high-quality performance video recordings of your current ensembles, be sure to bring those along when you meet your future students. This is a great way to let them learn more about you musically. This may also help get them excited to work with you and inspire them to aspire to a higher level of performance.

Be sure that everything about this interaction is positive. Let your future students ask you lots of questions. Be friendly. Be optimistic about your vision and goals for them in the program. Play something fun for them on your instrument and conduct them on a piece that they have been working on. Be sure to talk about fun community team-building events that you intend to do with them (picnics, bowling, movie nights, field trips, etc.). The idea is to make continuing in the program seem logical and appealing.

♫ Virtual Meet and Greet

If a physical meet and greet is not possible due to finances, location, or general travel challenges, see if you can do a virtual meet and greet. Many of the elements of a face-to-face meeting are possible to incorporate in a virtual meet-and-greet environment, other than conducting the ensemble. Going the extra mile to meet your future students can go a long way in developing your relationships with them.

♫ Promotional Video

Another option to connect with your future students is to create a short promotional video that is no more than five minutes. This video can include some of the following items:

- a video clip of you introducing yourself and giving a brief history of your background
- a short clip of you playing your instrument
- a short clip of you conducting your current ensembles
- a list of three experiences that you are looking forward to in the coming year

It is important to remember that even if everything goes exceedingly well in your meet and greets, you still may not win over every heart, and that is okay. Take comfort in the fact that some students will greatly appreciate your efforts in getting to know them.

♫ Welcome Letter to Your New Students and Families

In my experience, a welcome letter to your future students and parents can leave a positive impression on them before they even get to meet you in person. This can be a wonderful way to get students excited about what lies ahead instead of focusing on the current teacher they are about to lose. This also helps shift their focus away from how much the program they have known is going to change, and it can be reassuring to students who are on the fence about continuing in the coming year. They may find comfort in getting to know who you are and what your general philosophy will be for the program.

At the end of the day, making yourself available in this way has no real downside and several potential positive outcomes. The idea is to let your positive light shine as early on as possible.

Here is a sample welcome-letter template that can be tweaked or reworked however you see fit. Make it your own and send it to your future students and parents in whatever medium is best for your situation.

> Dear *[Orchestra/Band/Choir]* Families,
>
> My name is *[NAME]*, and I am excited to be joining the *[SCHOOL]* family, teaching *[SUBJECT]* in the 20*[XX]*–20*[XX]* school year. To tell you a little about myself, I graduated from *[UNIVERSITY]* with a major in *[DEGREE SUBJECT]* and later did my graduate studies in *[SUBJECT]* at *[UNIVERSITY]*. For the past *[NUMBER OF YEARS]* years, I have been teaching music at *[FORMER SCHOOL OR SCHOOLS]* in *[CITY OR CITIES]*. Teaching music is my passion, and I am truly looking forward to sharing it with all of the students in the program.
>
> I am also looking forward to experiencing new things, meeting new people, and learning more about what makes *[SCHOOL]* such a special community. I have known for many years that *[SCHOOL]* takes pride in offering their students the best possible music education, and I look forward to helping continue that legacy. The future of the *[Orchestra/Band/Choir]* program looks very bright. I am thrilled to be following in the footsteps of *[PREVIOUS TEACHER'S NAME IF APPLICABLE]*. *[S/he]* has set a high standard for the program that will allow us to reach greater

heights for years to come.

I teach from the perspective that it is my God-given responsibility to provide my students with the absolute best learning experience possible. While I don't expect my students to play like Itzhak Perlman or Yo-Yo Ma, I do strive to create a learning environment and classroom culture that drive all students to reach their personal best in the areas of musicianship, creativity, discipline, perseverance, flexibility, and the ability to work cooperatively with others. In my professional experience, environments like this don't happen by accident but rather are carefully crafted through strong classroom leadership and instruction, daily individual practice, private lessons, and meaningful performance opportunities. I am excited to help continue and add to the culture of excellence in the *[SCHOOL]* Fine Arts Department. The next school year will be filled with great music, exciting travel opportunities, and a very fun and engaging performance schedule.

For those of you whom I have not yet had the pleasure of meeting, I look forward to meeting you soon. For those I have met, thank you for the warm welcome.

With *[SCHOOL MASCOT]* pride,
Adrian Gordon

Getting Ahead

Summer can be a great time to get ahead and take care of some of the items that you might be too busy for once everyone is back on campus. Many school administrators will schedule end-of-summer meetings that may unintentionally set you back and begin to stress you out—unless you plan ahead. Consider coming in a few days early so that you have ample time to complete your personal goals without interruption. Even completing one or two personal goals before the madness of the school year begins can give you a sense of calm that you will need and want. Calmness will be a hot commodity to carry over with you into the beginning of the school year.

Keep in mind that vacation time is sacred, so consider limiting this type of activity to solely your transition year. Once you get settled and feel established in your new position, only use your summer vacation time for activities that will help you recharge.

Connecting with the Outgoing Director

In a perfect world, your transition to your new position would be perfect, and your music program wouldn't skip a beat during the move from one director to the next. In reality, we do what we can during transition periods to mitigate disruptions and bring consistency and stability to our students. One way to smooth out the changeover is to try to connect with the outgoing director and get a heads-up about issues that you need to know about before the school year starts.

Unfortunately, this isn't an option for some incoming directors because of the circumstances in which the position was vacated. You may not be able to communicate with the previous director if the program is new and you are the first, or if the previous director is uninterested or is no longer in contact due to firing or, in some cases, death. An introductory letter like the example I provided earlier may be the most important tool at your disposal if circumstances surrounding your new position mean you need to go in without any input from former music directors.

♫ What if there's no option to connect with an outgoing director?

In the event that there is not an open line of communication with the outgoing director, it's up to you to make the changes and adjustments you feel are necessary for the music program to flourish under your direction, lack of historical context notwithstanding.

Here are some examples of things you may face and need to take care of the summer before you start working with your new students:

- refiling unorganized music
- changing setup and seating based on electrical outlet accessibility
- ordering new music
- organizing storage
- updating your inventory (instruments, strings, accessories, etc.)
- cleaning and restringing instruments
- sending instruments in for repair
- hanging posters
- placing work orders or requests to have physical spaces repaired (lights fixed or changed, carpet cleaned, AC fixed, printers repaired, etc.)
- resolving student schedule changes and conflicts

Yearbook Study

Learning so many new names and faces at the same time during your transition can be overwhelming. When I found a yearbook in the days before starting my music director position at my new school, I found the opportunity to learn some new names and faces enormously helpful in the days that followed. Getting your hands on a recent yearbook is one of those tasks you can plan to accomplish if you can get on campus a few days earlier than the rest of the staff. Also, the yearbook:

- Allows you to develop professional relationships faster.
- Makes getting things done easier, since you know who to ask.
- Introduces you ahead of time to many of the students you'll meet on the first day, making classroom management much more efficient.
- Helps you demonstrate your interest in getting to know your new colleagues and students, which will make them feel special.

Learning about your new school from the yearbook can be a great way to make a great first impression on the members of your new community, as it will be taken as a sign of appreciation and respect. Online directories can be an option too if there happen to be employee pictures listed. Depending on the institution, there may only be email addresses and phone numbers listed, which won't really help you put faces to names. If all else fails, a current yearbook will be the best option.

Find a Mentor

Having a mentor professionally walk alongside you and guide you during your first couple of months to a year in a new place can be very helpful. This person can help you through procedural and school climate questions you may have on a day-to-day basis. If possible, try asking your new administration for a faculty mentor or faculty buddy if you are not assigned one. Have an attitude of gratitude toward them, and be sure to write down any valuable information they give you, whether it be logistic-, scheduling-, or personnel-related so that you can always refer back to it.

Reviewing Past Concert Program Booklets

Any advantage or added level of preparation you can give yourself as you walk into your new position will help. If you can review any past concert programs to see what the students' performance level and progression has been over the past year or more, do it. This will help you with the task of selecting new music for your students and will also allow you to review the program booklet traditions (section leader recognition, awards, acknowledgments, etc.) from the years past. From your review, you should also be able to get a better idea of whether you can add, take away, or improve the program booklet as a whole in the future. Overall, think of this task as another tool to help you clarify your vision and expectations for yourself and for the students in the upcoming year.

Beginning-of-the-Year Checklist

The beginning of a school year, especially a school year in a new position, can feel overwhelming. There are so many tasks to complete before your students return, but creating a beginning-of-the-year checklist can keep you from getting overwhelmed walking into your new environment.

In my first few years of teaching, it always seemed as if the beginning of the year was a mad dash to get organized and ready for students to return. I used to get stressed and frustrated because I would forget to do things or would run out of time to get things done. As I gained more experience, I realized that, just as in many other areas of life, creating a list can help you keep your thoughts and priorities organized. Around my fifth year of teaching, I started creating my beginning-of-the-year checklist, which helped me greatly. Following your own list as you move into your new position can be especially helpful. It can help you stay calm, organized, and strategic while you acclimate to your new environment.

Everyone's list will look different, but here is a sample of some of the things that I would do as I returned from summer break.

- check to make sure all students are in the correct ensemble
- set up gradebook with grade weights
- set up practice log dates in the gradebook
- conduct instrument repairs
- purchase all music on J.W. Pepper[2]
- set up folders to post e-print music
- clean up the room
- turn in all forms, handbooks, etc. required by the school
- create adjunct teacher schedule
- make an orchestra dates calendar for parents and students
- pay professional membership dues
- enter students' names in the music performance assessment online site
- print practice guide sheets to go over with students during the first week of school
- create a seating chart for each ensemble
- create instrument rental agreements

Try creating your own beginning-of-the-year checklist that can be edited each year to suit your needs. This list should only have the items that need to be completed at the very beginning of the year and that are most important to you. Not only will this list help you to be more effective in tackling your priorities and responsibilities, but it will also put your mind at ease and help you free up mental space to focus on being more engaging and creative for your students.

---

[2] J.W. Pepper, accessed April 9, 2022, https://www.jwpepper.com/sheet-music/welcome.jsp.

1. List some of the questions that you would like to ask the outgoing director.

   _____

2. In what ways do you intend to connect with your future students?

   _____

3. Whom can you ask to be a mentor in your new community?

   _____

4. What questions do you want to ask your mentor or colleague about the position and school community?

   _____

5. What does your beginning-of-the-year checklist roughly look like?

   _____

CHAPTER 4

"Takin' Care of Business" by Bachman-Turner Overdrive

Taking Care of Yourself Physically, Musically, Mentally, and Emotionally

S elf-care is the most important guiding principle to have at the forefront of any transition. Whether you are starting from scratch, rebuilding, or maintaining an already great music program, it is important to set boundaries for yourself so that the work doesn't become overwhelming. There will always be documents to sign, names and faces to learn, things to organize, gradebooks to update, parents to respond to, faculty meetings to attend, and lesson plans to develop. The work never stops, and it never will if you don't let it. The old adage "Rome wasn't built in a day" should now be truer than ever. No matter what circumstance you are walking into, the totality of it cannot be overhauled in just a short time. Your path should look more like a marathon than a sprint. Remember, constant exhaustion is not a badge of honor— it is a sign of health problems to come.

Physical Health

Here are several ideas to remember about your physical health during your transition:

- **Take breaks and keep your body moving.**
  - Remember to take breaks when working for long stretches at a time. (Many smartwatches have a "time to stand up and move" function already built in.)[3]
  - Stand up, stretch, breathe, walk around, and get some fresh air. Your body needs this! We can sometimes become very sedentary, working behind computers or sitting at our desks. By keeping your body moving, you will keep your mind alert and your blood flowing. Think of these breaks as a quick refresher so that you are better able to take on all of your tasks.

- **Use the restroom.**
  - It may sound ridiculous, but sometimes as educators we get so busy that even using the bathroom needs an appointment. Don't ignore your needs and potentially bring on health problems. Ask for help or class coverage so that you can make using the restroom a priority. Defy the chaos and put your health first.

- **Eat well.**
  - As busy as we get tying up loose ends, our food choices sometimes get pushed down to the bottom of our priority list. Don't let this happen! Make time to make smart, healthy choices about how you fuel your body. Plan ahead and pack some healthy snacks. You'd put

---

[3] "7 Best Smartwatches with Sedentary Reminder for an Active Lifestyle," Wearholic, accessed April 9, 2022, https://wearholic.com/smartwatch-with-sedentary-reminder/.

gas in your car if the fuel light came on—well, healthy food is the fuel that keeps your body running. Make sure you take care of your body.

- In my experience, I have found that having a stash of healthy snacks (fruit or vegetables) at my desk is helpful. No matter what foods you pick, having them available will mean you don't sacrifice healthy choices in the name of being too busy.

- **Don't lose sleep over it.**
  - Not only is a good night of sleep essential to your physical health, but it is essential for you to be able to do your job effectively. There were many nights my mind would wander and keep me awake for hours when I was supposed to be sleeping. Don't give up your sleep to a wandering mind. Write things down. If ideas or issues are swirling around in your head, write them down and leave them on the list. Your sleep is sacred!

Musical Health

Being ever-improving musicians is an important element that makes us effective music educators. We are also lifelong learners who seek to better understand the world around us by sharpening our professional skills and continuing to progress on our own instruments. It is important to stay focused on our own musical health in the midst of all the demands that our profession throws at us. Here are several ideas to remember about your musical health during your transition:

♫ Don't be the out-of-shape health-and-fitness coach on your instrument!

As a musician, no matter what instrument you play, it is important to stay connected to it and continue to play on a regular basis. It was always interesting to me the way people I would meet for the first time at casual gatherings, as well as many of the parents of my students, thought that the basis of my job as a music educator was solely to sit and play along with the students on my instrument all day long. I always wished that to be true, but in reality, that was the furthest thing from the truth. Between the administration, parent and student concerns, emails, phone calls, meetings, grading, and instrument repairs, playing and practicing on my instrument seemed to be the last thing on my mind for a long time.

What I didn't realize was that not being connected to my instrument, along with the process of disconnecting from the familiarity of my old position, had a profound effect. The rate and depth of change in your transition can sometimes be overwhelming. It helps to have a mental and emotional anchor reminding you who you are: a musician.

It wasn't until I heard someone talk about the optics of an out-of-shape health-and-fitness coach teaching a health-and-fitness class that a light bulb went off in my head. This is when my own practice priorities began to come into focus. Though the comparison is somewhat inartful, it was just a reminder, a harsh one, that it is important to emulate what you want your students to pick up and learn from you.

This is not to say that every music teacher needs to be ready to perform at Carnegie Hall but rather that every music educator should actually be a musician. Musicians play and practice on their instruments. No amount of lecturing can replace the experience of you picking up your instrument and modeling phrases, expressivity, dynamics, rhythms, fingerings, etc. Playing your instrument is not only beneficial to your musical mental health but also an integral part of being the best music educator you can possibly be.

So what does a priority shift look like? For me, it was simple. I started to incorporate small chunks of practice time into my days. If I could only squeeze in five minutes, then that's what I did. Practicing became more about the journey and less about the destination. It was more about progress and less about perfection.

I would also be sure to play the violin as much as I could with my students during rehearsal, if possible. I would even practice a few scales during transitions between classes. Sometimes I would play a pop song that was caught in my ear on a given day. Sometimes I would simply improvise over a blues progression. Sometimes I would play my students' music from the score that was right in front of me because I only had five minutes to play before my next class was coming in. It wasn't pretty, and it definitely wasn't worthy of a major concert hall performance, but it was real and manageable, and it kept me connected to my violin and music in general. Most importantly, it was well worth my time and helped keep me feeling like a musician.

Your practicing schedule might look different from mine, but the important thing is to not give up on playing your instrument in favor of paperwork and administrative tasks. Those things will never go away, but your muscle memory and technique on your instrument will. As you move into your new position in your new school, it will be easy to get lost in the sea of things to accomplish. Just remember that being and remaining a musician is a strong part of your professional identity.

♬ "But I'm not a string person" / "But I'm not a band person" / "But I'm not a choral person ..."

Sometimes, the general public doesn't quite understand specialization within our field. To them, one musician is just like another, and band, strings, and choir seem interchangeable. While there are commonalities in how we understand and interpret music, the methods and techniques we use to go about *making* music could not be more different. As music educators, we are sometimes "voluntold" to take on a new class that doesn't necessarily fall under our area of musical expertise. Sure, you might've taken a semester of technique class in that other instrument during college, but it never made you feel nearly accomplished enough to teach that subject.

So, what do you do? Here are some practical ideas to consider if you find yourself in this position:

- If you can sneak away from the podium to play along on your secondary instrument with your students, do it! One of the best ways to get better is to play along with your students. This will also give you insight into the difficulties they are having with the music and help you become a more sensitive and intuitive teacher.

- Be intentional about learning at least the very basics of each instrument in the ensemble, focusing especially on those you are unfamiliar with teaching. Start yourself off in a beginner book. Try moving at the pace of one to two months per instrument. Once you work your way through all of the instruments, pick the one you like the best and work consistently at progressing to at least an intermediate level.

- In many cases, expert level does not have to be attained in order to pass on knowledge to students. Even staying 10% ahead of your students at any given time will suffice.

- Remember, you are a teacher and a lifelong learner, so you instinctively look to understand the world around you. You will grow and learn as time moves on.

- Use your principal instrument (whatever it may be) initially to demonstrate intonation as well as rhythmic and melodic lines, until you begin to feel proficient on a secondary instrument.

- Consider taking at least one private lesson from an accomplished player on your secondary instrument. Be sure to ask a lot of questions and take as many notes as possible.
- YouTube or any other video streaming platform services can be extremely helpful. Search for beginner start-up videos and play-along videos to help you practice.
- Watch master classes online to pick up terminology, ideas, and pointers about a particular instrument.
- Have student leaders model correct posture, technique, phrasings, and rhythms to help take some of the pressure off yourself.
- Contact the closest university to see if any music education majors (whose principal instruments are a part of the ensemble you are teaching) would like to gain some experience running sectionals with students.
- If you are working with elementary or middle school ensembles, ask the high school director to come in and do a clinic in the fall and spring. Not only will this give you and your students some more musical insights, but it will also encourage your students to keep pressing ahead and give the other director an opportunity to recruit for their program.

♫ Professional Development

As you grow into your new position, it is also important to try to recharge your professional music batteries. The list of demands that is being thrown at you on a daily basis tends to take a quiet toll on you.

During my transitions into new music programs, I infused as much passion, energy, and excitement as I could into my role. Before long, positive changes in attitude, culture, and performance in the program emerged. However, the proverbial fire that I was trying to light within my new surroundings came at a heavy cost in the form of professional exhaustion. By the end of the first nine weeks, I felt as though every drop of creativity, innovation, and, indeed, music had been wrung out of me. This can happen to many of us as we get caught up in the excitement of our transitions. In the midst of all the changes, we sometimes don't realize how hard we are working.

I realized that if I, or anyone else in a similar situation, wanted to have longevity in a new position like this, there would have to be very intentional efforts to combat the high levels of professional exhaustion in a meaningful way. This is something we really all must do as music educators at every step of the way in our music education careers.

One of the ways we can combat our professional exhaustion and recharge is to attend professional development conferences. It was a blessing that my current school had a growth mindset and was a strong proponent of investing in professional development for their teachers. This was a saving grace and one of the reasons I didn't burn out. During all of my transitions between jobs, I was fortunate enough to attend professional development music conferences for a few days at a time. Attending these was vital to my musical and professional health for a few reasons:

- I was away from my school and music program. A little distance can go a long way.
- I was surrounded by other like-minded music educator professionals.
- I was surrounded by wonderful music ensembles and was able to listen to great music (practice versus pleasure).
- I was learning something new to help make me a better music educator.

If possible, try to attend professional development conferences at least once per year. Even if the professional development you pursue is virtual, it is important to keep your teaching practices and musicianship current and fresh. You also need an environment like this to help refill your musical tank, so to speak. Being around like-minded individuals who are all working toward the common goal of being the best music educators that they can be for their students is reinvigorating. If travel budgets are an issue for your particular school, look into doing webinars. Although they don't have the same feel as physically being in a professional development conference, they help feed your musical tank with inspiration.

In this day and age, you also have easy access to teacher support group pages or professional learning communities on social media. These outlets are great resources for learning, sharing, and commiserating with other professionals in your field, as well as gaining real-time professional development ideas any time of the day.

Mental and Emotional Health

Failing to take care of your mental and emotional health can prevent you from feeling like a whole person, let alone an effective music educator. Like all things in life, you have to find the balance in all the activities in your life to give yourself a sense of peace. Don't be afraid to take a step back to find balance and perspective. Guard your heart, mind, and personal time vigorously from the stresses of your job during your transition. Remember to never let your workflow take over your mental and emotional stability. And if your circumstances become too much at any given time, don't hesitate to talk to a mental health professional who can help you along your journey. Here are some practical ideas to consider to help you protect your mental and emotional health as you transition into your new position:

♫ Giving Yourself Grace

As you walk through your transition, it is good to be positive, have a good outlook, and set high expectations. But sometimes things don't go exactly according to plan. Our circumstances may very well not meet our expectations. Our students may not be moving as fast as we would like. The job may be harder than it appeared to be at the outset. Maybe you haven't made the connections you thought you would have made with colleagues. Whatever the imperfect case may be, give yourself grace! Don't be too hard on yourself. Accept and embrace where you are and give yourself the freedom to adjust to the unknown demands that you are just discovering. Placing too much pressure on yourself can be self-defeating, obscuring the critically important fact that any profession working with children is never an exact science. Be kind to yourself, and remember that your aim should be progress instead of perfection.

♫ Music Appreciation

As funny as it may sound, during my last transition, I had to rediscover the fact that I loved music. That might sound very strange, coming from a musician, but I'm not talking about loving music in a professional or pedagogical way but rather in an everyday kind of way, just enjoying listening to and discovering great new music. It can be easy to get caught up in the daily pedagogy of music that, in and of itself, is rewarding. But this is not the same as an aesthetic appreciation for music. If I had to think of a simple way to phrase it, I would look at it as "practice versus pleasure".

To help reignite my own connection to music during my transition, I made it a point to spend some time each day listening to something old that I liked, as well as something brand new. Opening my ears and my mind daily helped me rediscover music as something more than just a teaching tool, more like reconnecting with an old friend.

Music appreciation is an important concept to wrap our heads around during a job or school transition, and the rewards of preserving our uncomplicated enjoyment of music can benefit anyone at any stage in their music education career. You already know the power of music in your own life. Use it!

As you settle into your new role, you'll likely find yourself in the midst of very busy days and weeks. In the middle of all that business, remember to listen to great music regularly to help relieve tension and bring about mental and emotional relaxation. Attend recitals and concerts of musicians you enjoy listening to. Strive to keep your music profession from becoming a source of stress that makes you forget how enjoyable music can be aesthetically. Instead, let music be a source of relief.

♫ Sitting in Your Car

We all have low points at times throughout the day at work. Sometimes removing yourself completely from your campus and classroom can be refreshing. Your car can act as your home away from home. Try sitting in your car from time to time when you have a break. Take a few minutes and turn on the AC, kick your shoes off, and listen to your favorite relaxing song, say a prayer, do a devotional, or simply sit and enjoy the silence. Sometimes it only takes a few minutes of intentional relaxation to feel recharged for the rest of the day.

♫ Leaving Early

Pick at least one day a week where you leave right when school gets out and don't take any work home with you. Use this time to do something for yourself (going to the gym, reading, napping, watching TV, meeting a friend, spending time with family, etc.). Try to leave some time and energy in your day at least once a week to take care of yourself and do something meaningful for you.

♫ Taking a Day Off

We all receive sick and personal days throughout the school year to use when we need them. If possible, try to use two of your days throughout the year for mental health rest. Consider taking one in the fall and one in the spring. I have found that it can be beneficial to use them after a major concert that you have put on. Your mind and body need time and space to recuperate after such intense preparation with your students. Take advantage of the days you are given and use them to benefit your mental and emotional health. Your body will thank you for the rest.

♫ Taking a Temporary Change of Scenery in Where You Teach During the Summer

As you move into your new role, you may find yourself professionally exhausted. Building a new culture centered around your vision requires a lot of energy and can sometimes feel discouraging. Realize that even if you make significant strides in seeing your vision through to fruition, this will be more like a journey than a race. It will be an ongoing and evolving process that will eventually yield great returns as you see the student culture become more and more engaged with the possibilities of their music education experience. The emotional cost of encouraging, inspiring, motivating, and demonstrating to students who may not yet share your vision or understand your passion for your discipline can be high.

In my experience, working short stints at a summer music program, with its requisite change of pace and new scenery, had an invigorating and positive effect on my well-being. Most of the students who enroll in summer music programs tend to have a deeper appreciation for music than most, and you may find that the number of students who are looking to have a fun, short, great musical experience (with fewer strings attached than your normal gig) outweighs the number that don't. This can be rejuvenating for you.

It can be easy to get discouraged by the daily grind of the job and begin to believe that your vision may never come alive. If you are coming into a situation that is less than ideal in your new job, it's easy to become distracted with the shortcomings of your new environment instead of the possibilities and potential for positive change that you represent. It's also easy to become disenchanted with slower-than-expected progress in your transition. In some cases, you may feel that the majority of students studying music in your program are unengaged or simply uninterested in the vision you are offering. Changing your teaching scenery can serve as a reminder that there are students who derive deep satisfaction from playing their instruments and furthering their music education. It can also afford you the opportunity to see successes that you long for with students in a more informal setting that doesn't require the same expectations as a normal school year.

♫ Family

*Bonus Track: "We Are Family" by Sister Sledge

One of the most important things you can do as you transition into your new position is to protect your family time. The demands of the job will continue to bombard you, no matter how organized and efficient you are. There will always be more to do! However demanding the responsibilities become in your new position, it is important to remember that your family members need you the most. They should come first.

When you consistently borrow time away from your family, you are actually training the community around you to acknowledge that you are always available and that no part of your time is sacred. If you don't establish firm boundaries around your family time, some people around you will come to expect that you give up extra time with your family to finish or fix loose errands or emergencies. This is not okay, and it will leave you bearing the brunt of a stressful situation.

Set expectations early. Discuss with your family members what boundaries are important to them and how you can achieve them. Be unavailable after hours. Return emails during school hours only. Be unyielding with regard to protecting your family and personal time.

This is not to say that there won't be legitimate emergencies or issues that you attend to on occasion. This is particularly true around concert season or the time leading up to field trips. Try to anticipate emergencies you will encounter and plan ahead. This will look different for everyone, but for the most part, protect your personal time and try to remember the old saying "A lack of planning on your part does not necessitate an emergency on mine."

At the end of the day, remember that, in most cases, you are not getting paid any extra to be consumed by your position and be away from your family after hours.

As professionals, we also must consider that not only is it unfair to your family members to get the short end of the stick when it comes to your attention and energy, but it is unfair to you as well. You will need to recharge your batteries by being around your family members who love and care about you. Ideally, your family members offer solace. They are confidants whom you can turn to for encouragement and advice. They are also an important reminder of what matters most in life. They will help keep you grounded and make you a more balanced professional.

You have a unique role in your family that can only be filled by you. Whether it's your smile, your jokes, your stories, your affection, your singing, your dancing, your laughing, your playing, your attention, your hugs, your encouragement, or whatever it is that makes you special to your family, let your family members get the best parts of you. No matter what your family looks like, remember that *you* need your family, and your family needs *you*!

1. How can you improve your physical health with relation
    to your job?

    _____

2. How can you improve your mental health with relation to
    your job?

    _____

3. How can you improve your musical health with relation to
    your job?

    _____

4. How can you improve your family relationship with rela-
    tion to your job?

    _____

5. What tips or ideas would you like to explore to help main-
    tain or improve your mental and emotional health?

    _____

CHAPTER 5

"It's So Hard to Say Goodbye to Yesterday" by Boyz II Men

Letting Go of Your Former Role

L etting go of a former position and identity can be harder for some than others. If you are not careful, you can hinder your development and progress in your new community by not completely letting go emotionally. Your focus and energy can only be divided into so many different directions, and your priority needs to be the transition into your new position.

At the beginning stages of my third transition into a new school, the hook from the theme song of the TV show *Cheers* was constantly running through my head:

> *"Sometimes you wanna go, where*
> *everybody knows your name."*

Having been at my former school for 13 years, emotionally letting go of my position was much harder to do than I had thought it would be. I knew I was leaving to improve the situation for my family and myself, but my job had become so much of who I was. While no place is perfect, I had many fond memories of my time there. I think of it as my proverbial second coming of age. I learned a lot during my tenure at my first school. I became a better musician, teacher, and composer because of the relationships that I formed there with colleagues and students.

As I started working at my new school, I began to realize that nobody knew or really cared about what I had accomplished prior to my arrival. I was starting over and had to come to the realization that my past experiences and successes were much more relevant to my former students. The goodwill I had accrued with them would not roll over to my new community. I was alone with a head full of ideas, traditions, and practices, with nobody to understand or appreciate them. This was unexpected and took a little bit of time to adjust to. As successful as I perceived myself to have been in my previous job, it no longer mattered as I stepped into my new role.

This is an important aspect of your transition to expect and understand. Assume that nobody will know any of your successes that you have had over the years. Don't let this discourage you or make you want to give up; let it humble you and push you to do the hard work of building great relationships with your new community. Remember that your professional identity will look different than it did with your old community, and that is okay.

Credit Where Credit Isn't Due

A scenario that might arise as you settle into your new position (especially if you have left a strong and vibrant program in your former position) is that your successor may unavoidably take a lot of credit for the procedures, systems, and training that you have poured into your former students of that program. Maybe this doesn't bother you. Maybe you don't think twice about what you left behind. Those who do feel bothered by this, however, can feel sensitive or raw about it, particularly if their new program is behind their expectations and will take a significant amount of time to move forward in a direction that they find suitable.

Circumstances like these should also remind you to emotionally let go of what you left behind and focus on your transition into your new community. Be positive and continue to root for your successor's success, even when it is hard to do so. Our own success should never be predicated on someone else not succeeding. You never know if you may find yourself in a similar situation where you are taking credit for an already established program. In your own transition, you will especially want people like your predecessor rooting for you. Remember, it's all about the long-term success of the students in which we have invested. If they're successful, then the profession as a whole continues to succeed, which is good for all of us. The field of music education calls us all to provide students with an experience and journey that transcends any single teacher. Let that be your focus.

Final Decisions

As you flesh out your transition on a day-to-day basis, it is important to remember that moving on was a personal decision you made and will have both positive and negative outcomes. Take ownership of that decision, regardless of your current circumstances. As you settle into your new position, one of the best pieces of advice you can receive is to stay positive and keep moving forward.

If you haven't already, then, with an open and humble heart, mentally prepare yourself for the new experiences you will have by emotionally letting go of what once was and embracing the journey ahead. Think positively and know that you will become a better musician and teacher because of the relationships that you will form with new colleagues and students. This will take time, but from this point on, the only direction you should be looking is forward.

Letting Go of Your Former Students

♫ Cutting Ties

As hard as it was for me to leave my old school, it was also important for me to cut ties with former students, at least temporarily, for a couple of reasons. First, it can be very emotionally taxing to be working hard in a new environment and not see the results that you were expecting—yet. For me, I did not want to be seeking affirmation and reliving good times with the families whom I had worked with for many years, the ones that I had chosen to depart from. I knew I needed to take ownership of my decision to leave my old school. I also needed to start focusing on building relationships with my new students. I knew that my heart could not be in two places at the same time, even symbolically.

This did not mean that I implemented a strict radio silence policy with my former students and parents when they reached out to ask legitimate questions regarding music (recommendations, documents, questions, etc.). Don't feel as if you have to do that either. Just be sure to keep your conversations professional and stay away from gossip, critiques, comparisons, or complaints about your successor's new program. This is for everyone's benefit.

♫ Visitations

It is vital to remember that you need to keep moving forward with a positive attitude in your transition to your new job instead of physically revisiting the parts of your life that need to remain in your past. Visiting your old students and colleagues can emotionally hinder you from moving forward, as it has a way of drawing your focus away from continuing with the hard work of building connections with your new students. This is especially true if you are transitioning into a situation that is not all that you thought that it would be.

In the midst of all the transitional demands of my fourth job, I honestly began to desire the musical connections I had with my former students in my old school. The new job was harder than I had realized, and I wasn't making as much progress as I had thought I would be at that particular point in time. These feelings were not helpful at the time, because they drew my focus away from continuing with the hard work of building connections with my new students and subconsciously made me second-guess my decision to leave in the first place. This also would have been highly disruptive to my former students and my successor, as they were forging their own special, new bond. Though it would have been very easy to go back for a quick visit to reaffirm my own sense of value as a music educator, I didn't, and it was important that I didn't. I needed to remember that the relationships with my former students were not forged overnight, and the relationships with my new students wouldn't be either.

It was at times like these that I wish I would have had someone to remind me that despite my current discouragement and circumstances, I was selected for this new position because I am good at what I do. So let me explicitly remind you, you were selected for your new position because you have a particular set of skills that *you* are good at! These words should be a constant refrain in your head as you go about your days in your new position. Give yourself grace and believe, deep down, that you will eventually be building new bonds and success stories with your new students.

♫ Encouraging Former Students

Letting go of former students professionally can be very difficult, but in the end, it's beneficial for everyone. One of the most obvious things that you can do to help let go of your former students is to encourage them to stick with their music education, no matter what. Before I left my old school, as hard as it was, I made sure to always be encouraging to my soon-to-be-former students, who would occasionally voice their concerns about moving forward. I tried promoting goodwill toward their incoming director and continually asked the students to give the new director a fair chance. After I left, I had a few students who reached out to me to say that the program just wasn't the same.

"The new teacher doesn't play the same kind of repertoire," or "The new teacher doesn't grade the same way," they would say to me.

My response was always the same: "Give it time, and things will get better." I consistently made sure to encourage students to keep going in their musical journeys so that their music education was not contingent upon their relationship with me or, for that matter, their relationship with any one person.

♫ Drawing Comparisons

Whether you are walking into an environment that is a big step up or a big step down (in terms of performance level) from where you were, the important idea to remember is that it is essential to meet your students where they are and help them move forward. Once you determine the performance levels of the current students in your program, embrace where they are and reassure them of your intentions to help them reach the next level in their musical journey. Try not to compare your past and present groups to each other or pass judgment on either of them. If your current students are not as accomplished as your previous students, keep it to yourself, stay positive, and move forward. Drawing those comparisons can be demoralizing and counterproductive to your current students. It can potentially make you feel bad and unnecessarily make you second-guess your decision to have moved in the first place. It also draws your focus away from how you can help your current students improve on a daily basis. You will end up refocusing your attention on where you wish your students were at the present moment (and the frustrations that come along with it) instead of how you can best serve them to help them get there.

If your current students are further along than your previous students, don't let this reality make you become complacent. They will still need someone to guide them and help them move to the next level. Everyone has room to grow, and it is our job as music educators to make sure that happens. The idea is to meet your students where they are, no matter what level you find them at. Your goal for your students should be progress toward their personal best.

Whatever scenario you find yourself in, don't let comparisons hinder your progress with your students. Meet them where they are and keep moving forward!

Healthy Boundaries and What They Look Like

♬ Availability

As I said earlier, setting boundaries between your past and present is an important part of moving forward in your new role. Setting boundaries is important for a smooth transition between your old and new positions, but that doesn't mean I'm saying you should ignore your former students if they reach out to you with questions or to ask for help. If a former student genuinely needs help with something, being there for them is important.

Put yourself in the shoes of your successor when setting boundaries between your past and present positions. Be available to your former students for help with any information that pertains to the past that cannot be obtained anywhere else except through you, but make sure that you're not overstepping any boundaries or current lesson plans that might hinder your former students' development with their new director and your own development with your new students.

Practically speaking, I settled on the rule that if there was something specific that my former students needed, such as recommendation letters, performance documents, or answers to past performance questions, I was more than happy to help. If there were any questions or issues pertaining to the future (auditions, seating, or events), I left those to their new director out of respect. Setting these boundaries clears a path for you to move on and will benefit everyone.

♫ "Remi-listen" Only if You Must

If you are feeling discouraged as you come into your new role because the performance level of your students isn't as high as that of students in your previous position for whatever reason, then this section will be of great importance to you. During my last transition, this was my reality. I sometimes made the mistake of remi-listening. Yes, you read that word correctly. I define "remi-listening" as the act of reminiscing on past musical experiences by way of listening to music recordings. After getting worked up several times and realizing that I was causing myself more anxiety than peace by listening to old recordings of my students, I made it a point to try not to listen to them unless there was a legitimate educational reason. I would advise you to do the same, at least for a while or until you feel established in your new position.

This boundary will be particularly important if your current position is not meeting your expectations in terms of playing level. Remi-listening to past performances in this manner can bring about unnecessary anxiety. Instead, track and listen to performances of your current students. Listen critically for things that you can do better as a teacher to help your students improve. Also, be intentional about looking for growth in your students' playing and letting them know when and where you hear it.

♫ Visiting Hours Are Over

Making a clean break from your old position and not looking backward is an important part of transitioning into your new community. As I was getting acclimated to my new position, I made it a point to be absent from my old school. Specifically, I settled on not visiting the school or attending any events. Not only did I need time and space to focus and open up my heart to my new students, but my successor also needed space to build her own vision without me getting in the way. She deserved space to build relationships with the students without their hearts being tugged on by me showing my face. Note that this may be easier for some people than others, depending on the distance you are moving and the kind of working conditions and environment you are leaving behind.

Regardless of the terms that you left on, keep your distance from your old position and allow your heart and mind the time to settle into your new position. This will be beneficial for you and your new community, as well as the community you left behind.

♫ I'm Talking Old School

Sometimes we can unknowingly demoralize our new students with too much talk about our old positions. It may make them feel as if you never really left. People tend to hold on to first impressions, so it is important that we are clear and intentional in our messaging.

During my last transition, I tried very hard to not speak too much about my old school with my new students. If I did, it was short and sweet, and even then, I would sometimes hear grumblings. I didn't want my new students to feel as if they were being compared to my old students or that my heart was not fully present with them, so eventually I stopped mentioning the old school completely.

Try to limit your conversations about your old school with your new students so that it doesn't appear that you are more excited about what you left behind than you are about the experiences that are yet to come. Answer any questions your current students may have about your former school and students, but constantly assure them that you are there with them for the long haul.

1. **What part of your identity from your former position are you holding on to that might be preventing progress in your new position?**

   _____

2. **In what ways can you set healthy emotional boundaries to help you move forward?**

   _____

3. **What healthy boundaries have you already implemented during your transition? How has this helped you?**

   _____

   _____

4. **Are there additional healthy boundaries that have not been discussed that you would like to add to your personal list? How and why do you think they will help you move forward?**

   _____

   _____

5. **In what ways, if any, have you not let go of your former students?**

   _____

6. How can you go about changing this in a professional manner?

_____

_____

7. In what ways can you be intentional in connecting with your current students to show them that you care about their well-being?

_____

CHAPTER 6

"Change the World" by Eric Clapton

Types of Change to Expect in the Next Few Years

C hange is one of the very few guaranteed parts of life. It comes whether we want it to or not. Change can be positive, and change can be negative. Change can sometimes even leave us feeling indifferent. With a director transition in any music program, there is bound to be change, whether that change is big or small. Everyone has different ideas, methods, and philosophies, and music directors are no exception. The key for new music directors is to manage the change to the best of their ability.

In my experience, unmanaged change can lead to a lot of resistance—and sometimes avoidable conflict—from the people around you. This can happen even if that change is ultimately in your students' best interest. Here are some ideas to consider as you navigate through changes of all kinds in your new position.

Changing Directors

Comparisons between you and the former director are bound to happen. Try not to let the comparisons discourage you. You are a unique professional who has a lot to offer in your own right. Don't be afraid to respectfully push back when people compare your leadership style to that of your predecessor. You can simply state:

"While I appreciate what [*PREVIOUS TEACHER'S NAME*]_____ did for this program over the past several years, I am not them. I am my own person. There is always room for improvement, and I'd like to try something new that will be beneficial to every student."

Throughout my last transition to a new school, I realized that change was going to be hard for my new community. They were very fond of the previous director, and they missed him very much. No matter how much they wanted me to be like the previous teacher, it was never going to happen. Our perspectives and approaches to music education were different. We had different educational backgrounds. We had different levels of teaching experience. Our DNA was different!

Try not to take the comparisons personally. Focus on your efforts to provide the best musical experience for your students. Always look for better ways to develop new bonds with your current students. It is important to note that, in some cases, you are replacing someone special whom your new students loved. Seize the opportunity to connect with your new students and fill a void in their musical journey. Don't apologize for being you. Remember that, at the end of the day, you can *only* be you!

♫ No Gossip

Professionalism should be a key character quality to model for your students. Kids are learning from us all the time, even when we are not explicitly teaching from a prepared lesson plan. Your students are always watching, absorbing, and trying to make sense of the world around them, including the things you say and do as their teacher. Because of this reality as educators, it is important to remember that, as you push for change in your new program, you should never speak negatively about your predecessor or the way they used to do things. For that matter, there also shouldn't be any negative talk about any colleagues; choose your words carefully. Although negative talk can be very tempting in certain situations (especially if you come up against unfair comparisons), it is always best to stay professional, even if it feels as if the world is jumping down your throat for daring to do things differently than they had been done before. Continue to ask yourself the philosophical questions of "Who do I want to be for my students, and what do I want them to learn from me intentionally and unintentionally?"

If you are called upon to defend or explain certain decisions that you are making that are different from the way things were done before, make sure that your defense or explanations remain professional and focused on empirical and objective outcomes as much as possible, rather than on personal and emotional critiques of your predecessor.

♪ Changing Vision

One can only hope that the vision your predecessor held falls exactly in line with your own vision for the music program. If that is the case, consider yourself fortunate, and continue to do your best to uphold that vision and legacy of excellence that has been long established. For some, your arrival is the beginning of a change in the vision and direction of the music program.

Communicating your vision to your new community is one of the key actions you'll need to take to smooth the transition to your new school. This doesn't mean that everyone will agree to, or even care for, your new vision, but it creates an environment of honesty where all cards are laid on the table, and parents and students can decide whether your vision is something that they want to participate in. When I came to my school, I shared my vision for the program with the students, and to this day, it has not changed, because it's worked for me.

My vision is three-pronged, and it is as follows:

1. **Excellence:** Take pride in your music studies and strive for the highest levels, whether it be behaviorally, musically, academically, or in terms of performance.
2. **Dedication:** Set long-term goals musically, commit to playing for several years, and have the discipline to practice regularly.
3. **Community:** Create friendships and serve others through music.

These points were broad enough that I was able to meet at least a few expectations of every person currently in the music program. I was also able to ask students what they envisioned the music program looking like in the weeks, months, and years ahead. If there were great ideas that fell outside of what I had already cast, then I wouldn't hesitate to add them in. You can even add bits and pieces of your vision into your email signature so there is a constant reminder of your vision whenever there is correspondence between you and your students.

You can think of this as somewhat of a mission statement that holds your guiding principles and can always be referred to throughout the year. Communicate your vision with your students, parents, and administration. Be sure that, whatever your vision is, it is well thought-out and clear. Share it often. Explain when circumstances fall in line with the vision of the program and when they don't. Celebrate the moments when your vision is encapsulated in the students' stellar work. Sharing your vision creates a clearer path for you to lead and for students to follow.

♫ Students are dropping like flies! What do I do?

Being music educators offers us the ability to greatly influence our students. Because we work with students in a unique social and academic setting over many years, this allows for great relationships and bonds to be formed. Conversely, this environment also allows the opportunity for the rejection from students quitting to feel deeply personal.

The sting of rejection from students quitting can sometimes make you second-guess many of your decisions and interactions. If several students happen to quit your program at the same time, you may even question your effectiveness as an educator. Try not to take the small number of students leaving simply because of your arrival as a personal insult, but rather, look at it as an opportunity to establish a strong rapport with the remaining students. These students may have a greater influence than you in persuading defectors to return or in recruiting brand-new members. Word of mouth is a strong marketing tool, and you definitely want the students doing the marketing to have a vested interest in your program.

Some of the attrition you may see will be no fault of your own and purely based on students' circumstances and personal situations. However, some of the attrition you will see will, in fact, be personal. Be prepared for this. Even after trying your way of doing things, some may not take to your teaching style. It is important for you to remember that this still does not mean you are necessarily doing anything wrong. This may just mean that your way of doing things is *different*. Remember that different does not necessarily mean deficient; different simply means different.

Here are some important ideas to remember when you are feeling rejected due to students quitting:

- Maintain a professional, positive, optimistic, and pragmatic outlook, regardless of what comes your way.

- Don't take their decisions to quit personally. Look at it as an opportunity to develop stronger bonds with the students who choose to stay. Don't lose focus in serving the students who stay and enjoy your program.

- Remember that you will not be able to win everyone over to your vision. As the old expression goes, "You can't please all the people all the time."

- Don't apologize for being who you are. Remember, you can only stay true to who you are and do your best to serve your students as ethically and lovingly as possible.

- Be humble and eager to make the program better and more harmonious for everyone, if warranted.

- Trust in the effectiveness of consistent kindness and professionalism.

It is understandable that change can be difficult for students and parents, but whether we like it or not, the only thing that is constant is change itself. This means that those who are upset about the changes you make will have to find a way to cope with them. Not everyone will be on board, but as the old saying goes, you have to crack a few eggs to make an omelet.

In the interest of being introspective and having a growth mindset, sometimes it can be wise to take some time to reflect and recognize if there are any legitimate concerns that you can address and handle better. Welcome discussion about the direction of the program while taking students' personal music education goals into consideration. Compromise where you can without sacrificing your integrity or the integrity of the program. Be open to trying new things that may be a better fit than the way you are used to doing things. Be flexible. Expect students to adhere to the school code of conduct as well as your own classroom standards. No matter who comes and goes and what changes are taking place, demand excellence from yourself and your students.

♫ Laying the Groundwork to Change Minds

If the attitudes of the people around you are indifferent, or even flat-out negative, some groundwork will need to be laid to help your community buy into your leadership and vision.

During my last transition, it came to my attention that many parents and students were not very pleased with the changes that I was making within the program. They didn't like the fact that they went from rehearsing one or two days out of the week to rehearsing every day. They didn't like the fact that we would rehearse for the entire class period. They didn't like the fact that I was now requiring students to practice daily at home on their instruments for 15 minutes. They didn't like the fact that there were now graded assessments within the class. They felt as though the class was supposed to be fun—and by *fun,* they meant no accountability.

I assumed that most parents would welcome the push toward learning, excellence, and discipline, but I was certainly wrong. They just weren't used to the changes being made. Because the vision and cultural shift that I was ushering in were so different from what they were used to, there was a lot of pushback. Not used to rehearsing every day, the students would ask questions:

> "Why is he making us rehearse during class?"

> "Why is he making us practice at home?"

> "Why can't we go outside and play dodgeball?"

> "Can we watch movies instead of rehearsing?"

To my surprise, I also received a lot of passive-aggressive comments (as well as some outright aggressive ones) from parents:

> "You are just striving for excellence with the orchestra, and that's not what this is about. It's about exposure!" (This message was delivered while yelling.)

"My child always *used* to love music—until this year."

"The other teacher used to make things fun and play hip-hop and pop songs."

Eventually, most of the students and parents who were resistant to my curriculum had a change of heart when the students saw improvements in themselves and within the music program overall. Here are some practical tips that I used that can help you bring about change in the minds of resistant students and parents:

- Be patient.
- Be kind.
- Be helpful.
- Bring humor into your program (jokes, memes, etc.). Even the most driven of musicians can laugh during practice. Humor can be very disarming.
- Make your expectations clear on day one. Minimize any surprises for your students regarding what is expected of them. Spell everything out clearly in their syllabus and consider having the parents sign off on it.
- Win over your students. Remember to show the students that you care for them. Your pupils' parents are much more likely to be in your corner if their kids enjoy your class and appreciate your investment in them as people.
- Invite parents to help volunteer and chaperone at any events you hold. Their investment may translate into attachment.
- Regularly communicate the group accomplishments of the students in your program to the parents. It is more difficult for anyone to argue with your leadership when the success of the students is on public display. Their success should be neutral territory for all parties.
- Document conversations with difficult parents.

- Involve an administrator in any parent-teacher conference that you feel may not be respectful or productive. You are not a punching bag!

The bottom line is that you will never be able to please everyone with decisions that you make. You can only stay true to who you are and do your best to serve your students as ethically and lovingly as possible. It is also important to remember that you can't always control what happens to you, but you *do* have control over how you respond.

♫ Change and Accountability

It can be unsettling and frustrating for anyone when changes come out of nowhere and trip them up. As thoughtful and strategic as you'll want to be about the changes you're making, no change is completely seamless; therefore, you should establish a way for you and your students to clearly define what the changes are and then remain accountable once the changes are implemented. At the very least, be sure you level with your students about the changes you're making and, when possible, why you're making them. Afterward, you can even draft up a written list of the new things students can expect and add it to a syllabus or student contract that the students and parents can always refer to for clarity or when they have questions.

Clarity about the changes you're making in what's expected of students helps everyone stay confident and on track. Here are some ideas you can employ to help students stay accountable and responsive to your new expectations:

- Attach a grade to their accountability for the change or changes you are implementing.
- Begin a reward system to encourage your students to consistently adopt the new change.
- Establish a social contract about the implemented changes

that are discussed and agreed on by all the students.

Whatever change management tool you choose, the idea is that the changes are clearly discussed and that your students understand what's new for them and how you will hold them accountable to those changes.

♬ Change from Within

Any time you work to change or influence your students in a meaningful way, you will also find that your own professional life will evolve. When I headed into my most recent transition, I don't think I anticipated that reciprocity, even though I was specifically brought in to change the music program and culture. Before long, I noticed changes taking place in me; I began to grow as a musician and as an educator as a direct result of encountering new challenges in a new school. I was adapting my approach to meet my new students' needs. While I hadn't anticipated my own professional leveling up, these were all positive changes and lessons that only required a conscientious and humble heart to receive them.

Be open to the change that will happen within yourself. Be flexible! Continue to learn, grow, adapt, and improve in all aspects of your profession. Don't be too hard on yourself when your goals, ideas, and vision evolve to suit your professional circumstances. Your newest transition may not look exactly as you expected or resemble any that you've experienced before. Allow your heart and mind to be okay with this. You can only stay true to who you are and do your best to serve your students as ethically and lovingly as possible.

You may also be coming into your new position with a new set of personal life circumstances compared to what you were used to in your old position. The last time you handled a change in your professional life, your family situation might've looked different. Maybe you've gotten married, had children, gotten divorced or re-partnered, or encountered a change in health status since then. Maybe having your new position means you need to adjust to a new home or community in addition to your new role. For me, this looked like changes within my family. I had had children of my own between my previous transition and this one, which meant that this professional transition was a very different experience.

Time and circumstances had changed me and helped me realize that my family came first at all times, even in the midst of a professional transition. I knew that my next program-building phase was not going to look like the previous one. This is something that we all have to take into account. Though we employ the best pedagogical approaches in each and every classroom, no two transitions will look exactly alike, especially when personal life changes are thrown into the mix. Remember that your students are expected to grow emotionally, intellectually, and academically. There is no reason why any less should be expected of you.

This concept requires a deep level of introspection, patience, perseverance, and perspective. Take the time to acknowledge the areas that you have grown or matured in, and realize that this will affect the way you do things in the present moment. Program development may move faster or slower than before because time has granted you wisdom, experience, and, in some cases, new life priorities.

Don't be afraid to accept or invite change within yourself where it is warranted. **Be flexible and compromise where you can to promote healthy living, a smoother transition, and a strong working environment.** In the midst of all the life changes you may experience, remain steadfast and principled where it matters the most to protect the integrity of the music program as a whole.

1. **What life changes that affect your performance do you need to take into consideration as you transition into your new position?**

2. **In what ways can you adapt your professional life to accommodate the changes and circumstances in your personal life?**

♬ **Change in *How* vs. Change in *What*
(Don't Sweat the Small Stuff)**

*Bonus Track: "The Remedy (I Won't Worry)" by Jason Mraz

What happens if your tried-and-true methods, and the changes that you may be excited to introduce into your new community, prove impossible to implement? Or what if your ideas are flat-out rejected? Roadblocks will look different for everyone and will have different implications and different solutions.

Sometimes scheduling, facilities, policies, team preferences, or administrative preferences may be the obstacles that prevent you from advancing the ideas that you think will be beneficial to your students and your program. Even with extenuating circumstances looming, let these types of roadblocks guide you into a creative space that allows you to adapt your approach to best suit your students. As I said previously:

> *"Be flexible and compromise where you can to
> promote healthy living, a smoother transition,
> and a strong working environment."*

In my last transition, one particular roadblock came to me in the form of student-group travel restrictions. My previous school had thankfully offered the resources to afford overnight trips for the music program students to travel as a large group. In my experience, traveling together across the music disciplines (band, orchestra, chorus) created a strong community between the disciplines, and the experiences bolstered the department and made students want to attend that school just to be part of the music program. This wasn't how things worked at my new school, no matter how much I wished it were. Every performing arts discipline made their own travel plans that rarely overlapped, precluding any chance to build an interdisciplinary music community among my new students.

Was this change the end of the world? Absolutely not. For one thing, our students were incredibly fortunate to even have the opportunity to travel at all. I needed to gain some perspective and remember that *how* we were traveling was changing, but *what* we were doing—traveling for musical education—would continue.

Being flexible and understanding meant accepting that maybe the plans that I had envisioned would have to be a possibility for the future, or maybe not at all. *What* we were doing—music education—wasn't changing, but *how* we were doing it required me to adjust my expectations. Being flexible in this instance did not jeopardize my integrity or principles in any way. This was simply a matter of preference and tradition over which I did not need to start a battle.

Don't sweat the small stuff! Try to find areas that are different from what you are used to, and see if you can be flexible with how you approach them. It is also important to note that flexibility does not mean you need to roll over and be passive whenever there is a difference of opinion within your school. If you have a good idea, speak up and share it respectfully, but remember that it may not always be widely accepted. See if you can meet in the middle, or simply let some things go altogether, especially if they're not things that put your integrity and peace of mind in jeopardy.

So, what does entering a creative space and adapting your approach look like for you in practical terms? The possibilities are endless, but they can look like any of the following:

- Building after-school rehearsals into the calendar because of master scheduling conflicts
- Creating an early bird class to accommodate students who couldn't join your program otherwise
- Programming easier music due to time constraints and interruptions
- Starting students who are far beyond the program performance level and are in a mixed-level class on a secondary instrument

This list of challenges and creative solutions could go on forever and looks different for everyone. Whatever your challenge may be, the idea is to not let it rattle you and throw you off your game. Think fast and be creative. Remember that sometimes you don't need to change *what* you are doing, just *how* you are doing it.

1. **What are some practices you hold dear that you think you may be able to relinquish, or at least be flexible with?**

_____

_____

2. **What are some important changes that have been blocked for you for one reason or another? What creative detours can you take to accomplish these particular goals without overstepping your bounds?**

_____

_____

♫ **Unnecessary Change**

*Bonus Track: "Waterfalls" by TLC

Resist the urge to reinvent the wheel. Once you identify what's already working well, build on it. If there are policies or practices that have proven successful in the past, continue them. See if you can learn something new from what already exists. You may be surprised at what new ideas you can add to your repertoire. Building trust with your new students, keeping an open mind, and listening first and foremost should be your main goals. As the students get to know, like, and trust you more and more, you can begin to make incremental changes that you deem necessary. Here are some practical tips to consider:

- Maintain traditions if possible (social events, games, annual field trips, student awards, etc.). If there is a tradition that seems particularly disagreeable to you, make it a priority to phase it out over time.
- If possible, choose music repertoire you have already performed in the past, no matter what performance level you will be working with. This allows you to more easily match music to your students' playing ability and meet them where they are. This also opens up space for you to give more of yourself to your students musically without adding any unnecessary stress in the midst of learning names, abilities, school procedures, school culture, etc.

1. **What are some traditions that you have come into at your new school that you have embraced? What, specifically, did you learn?**

   _____

   _____

2. **What are some of the traditions you have come into that you are not excited about keeping but that may be more beneficial to either leave in place or slowly phase out?**

_____

_____

3. **If there is a practice or tradition that you do intend to phase out, is there a way you can do it incrementally?**

_____

4. **What are some pieces that you are already familiar with (at the level you will be teaching) that you will be able to easily teach your students?**

_____

♬ Changing Culture

*Bonus Track: "Waiting on the World to Change" by John Mayer

Your presence as music director will affect the culture of your new program. You're your own person with different ideas, approaches, and philosophies, so some changes will be inevitable. The main point to understand about changing or correcting the course and culture of a program is that these adjustments take time. In my experience, there tends to be a loose timeline with regard to a culture change taking root and the program becoming a reflection of you as a director.

> **Years One to Two:** Changing course and building relationships with students

> **Years Two to Four:** Reaction to changes/buy-in, recruiting and retention

> **Years Four to Five:** Outcomes and continuity

The change in culture, whether it is a slight shift or a major overhaul, must be meaningful and also incremental. Change for the sake of change can be self-defeating, and change that is too fast and broad can be overwhelming.

The best way to think about change management surrounding culture is by reflecting on the old children's story of the boiling frog. The premise of the story is that a frog is tricked into getting into some lukewarm water on a stove. The temperature is slowly raised to boiling, but the frog is much less aware of the change in temperature and therefore stays in the pot; if it had been placed directly in the boiling water, the frog would have jumped out. (This, of course, is a bit morbid as it relates to children, and I am not advocating for boiling our students.) What I *am* saying is that the students, parents, and administrators may be much more receptive to change if it is gradual and not as noticeable as a pot of boiling water.

It is helpful to map out the current realities of your program versus where you would eventually like to see the program end up. Then it is much easier to plot a step-by-step plan of action for getting there.

Here is a sample outline of an action plan to help with change management in your new position:

1. Identify what your circumstances are now.
2. Identify what you would like to see change.
3. Clearly write out what changes you will be making for students.
4. Settle on what tools you will be using to bring about change.
5. Choose a method to help keep everyone accountable for the changes.
6. Have a method of measuring, reflecting on, and drawing conclusions about the effectiveness and outcomes of the changes you have implemented.

My own obstacle to changing culture popped up immediately as I embarked on my last transition. When I first arrived at my new school, students would openly admit that they had never been required to practice or take their instruments home before. They may have been *asked* to take their instruments home and practice, but they openly admitted that they didn't do so.

Students would say things like this:

> "We would only practice a lot the day of the concert to make sure we didn't completely bomb."

> "Our concerts were embarrassing because we would never practice."

> "I never used to invite my parents to my concerts because we wouldn't practice, and it sounded bad."

This wasn't what I wanted to hear, but it was the truth. This is where I was: identifying the current circumstances (step 1).

The next step was to think about where I wanted to be and how to get there (step 2). I wanted to prioritize this change in practice culture and see students involved in daily practice over the course of the school year. I wanted a thriving program filled with highly motivated students who loved music-making and practicing as much as I did. I wanted to have a top-notch program where students were reaching for their personal best on a daily basis. Realistically, I had to check my grand ambitions at the door and start prioritizing one step at a time. The next thing I had to do was get the students practicing on their instruments.

There was no standing policy in place to help my students be accountable for their work. My first instinct was to tell them flat-out to just go home and practice. But I needed to be much more thoughtful and specific while emphasizing quality of practice over quantity of practice. Instead of saying, "Go home and practice for an hour," I had to manage the change and expectations and be more strategic about the implementation of a practice policy.

Ultimately, I wanted to be able to say to the students, "Go home and practice like this ..." Knowing that this was not a part of their music culture, I decided that I needed to give them much more clearly defined guidance on the proper way to practice. To facilitate the students developing their independence and effectiveness in practicing, I ended up writing out the daily practice procedures and expectations for them so they always had a document to refer to (step 3).

The strategic tool that I used to help bring about change in the culture behind practicing and to introduce more accountability was practice logs. I understand that the verdict is still out on the efficacy of practice logs, but for me, this was one of the most thoughtful ways I could start promoting a culture of strong and disciplined music-making that involved the parents, students, and myself. Are practice logs a perfect system? Absolutely not. But this was a tangible and practical method that I chose to help bring about change (step 4).

My next step was to implement a growth-mindset system of playing assessments to help students stay accountable to the changes being made (step 5). Students were now required to take weekly or biweekly playing assessments with me (in quartets, quintets, or sections), depending on the weekly schedule. All students, no matter their level, were required to reach an 80% grade before a performance, out of respect for me, themselves, each other, and their audience. The caveat was that they were allowed to retake a playing test as many times as they wanted throughout the quarter and leading up to their performance. This policy meant that I was taking on a more active role in helping them improve, and I made myself available to the students every day before and after school. Playing assessments are an example of a strategic tool to bring about change in the culture.

As uncomfortable as it was at times to implement these changes, by the end of the school year, I was able to see measurable improvements in the performance ability and grades of my students (step 6). Scale performance improved, overall tone quality of the students improved, and repertoire performance and understanding of different pieces in the same grade level improved. This was encouraging and helped me forge ahead with bringing about positive change in the program.

Whatever change you are committed to bringing to your new program, make sure that it suits your vision and that you map out the realities of where you currently are with your program versus where you would eventually like to see the program end up. Have a step-by-step action plan with practical tools and a time frame to see results of the changes you are implementing. Think about a way (formal or informal) to measure the efficacy of the changes you are implementing. This will allow you to be flexible and tweak, improve, or change your strategies depending on what works best for your students. You can't change the world overnight; you can, however, bring about meaningful change over time without immediately bringing the pot to a boil.

1. **What are the most meaningful and pressing cultural changes that you would like to see happen this year? Why?**

   _____

2. **How incremental will these changes be (weeks, months, years)?**

   _____

3. **What is your plan of action to make these changes come to fruition over time?**

   _____

I have included a practice guide in this chapter that is flexible and can be adjusted to any teacher's needs and preferences. Feel free to copy it, add to it, take away from it, or trim it down. Keep in mind that there may not be an established culture of practicing where you are going, and a written document (that you go over with your students) that spells out the process may be a beneficial tool.

45-Minute String Player Practice Schedule Guide

This is a general outline of what your practice time should look like. You may need to adjust (add minutes or take away minutes) according to your particular needs.

1. Set up. (Setting up is not included in your practice time.)
2. Tune.
3. Strategize practice. Make notes in your music with a pencil.
4. Sight-read.
5. Play by ear.

General Tips

- Rosin your bow.
- Carefully tune your instrument before beginning your practice.
- Establish what you will target in your practice time and how you will go about improving by the end of your practice session. Be sure to use your practice tools (metronome, tuner, SmartMusic, audio recordings, etc.).
- Establish whether your difficulties are originating in the right hand, left hand, or both.
- Try to practice in front of a mirror so that you can see any physical irregularities in your playing (posture, left-hand frame, bow hold, bow placement, bow angle, bow distri-

bution, etc.)

- S-I-S-R-A (**S**top, **I**solate, **S**low down, **R**epeat five times perfectly in a row, **A**dd it back in). This is the way you should practice any and all difficult passages.

Minutes 1–5

- Warm up by playing the scale related to the piece you are working on. (There should be no intonation issues during this time. Use a tuner if necessary.)

Minutes 5–30

- Practice with a metronome, starting very slowly and increasing the increments by five clicks after playing through at each particular tempo perfectly.
- Circle accidentals.
- Circle notes that you forget have a sharp or flat sign from the key signature.
- Write in bowings.
- Write in fingerings.
- Write in counts of rhythmically tricky measures.

Minutes 30–40

- Practice sight-reading. Read anything and everything. Consider using the sight-reading exercises books 1–10 on SmartMusic. (Start with book one and work your way forward.) *Do not move on from an exercise unless you get at least a 90%.

Minutes 40–45

- Have fun and play something that *you* want to play by ear.

CHAPTER 7

"Happy Together" by The Turtles

Building Community

As you begin establishing yourself in your new position, be sure that community building is at the top of your list of priorities. A cohesive social fabric between the students in the program will create a deeper sense of investment and accountability toward each other. This will also help create a strong layer of trust in you as their leader because you have helped foster such a positive and enjoyable atmosphere for their music education journey.

Always strive to develop a professional, yet caring relationship with your students. Pay attention to whether students feel as though they can talk to you about a wide range of topics, such as music, sports, their athletic games, difficulties in other classes, food, and vacations. During my own transitions, I have found that one of the outcomes of emphasizing community in a music program was that most students were eager to share the interesting and sometimes not-so-interesting parts of their lives with me. Even when there were times when I felt too busy to listen, I always did, and I never regretted it. Students' ability to come and talk to you about anything should be one of many barometers of the social health of the music program.

It is also worth pointing out that I would consider the students' ability to speak to each other another barometer of the social health of the program. This is why it is important to regularly schedule and promote team-building events throughout the school year. Efforts to build community and convey your care for your students do not have to be overthought or overly complicated. Here are some simple and practical suggestions:

- Share parts of your life that are important to you when possible. This humanizes you.
- Ask your students what their expectations are for their music education.
- Always offer to be available after school to help students who need it, giving your students extra help with their music or even with other subjects. This is especially valuable if you have another academic expertise where students could benefit from hearing a different perspective on a subject.
- Don't be afraid to have planned or impromptu jam sessions with students.
- Tell your students music jokes to get them laughing. (Dad jokes are the truth!) Here's one of my favorites: "My wife asked me to stop singing 'I'm a Believer' by The Monkees because she found it annoying. At first, I thought she was kidding. *'But then I saw her face …'*"
- Regularly ask your students how they are doing.
- Ask your students how their extracurricular activities are going.
- Attend a student sports game. (You may not be able to attend them all, so see if there is a sport that a lot of your students have in common.)
- Plan a kickball game or picnic that can be fun and laid-

back for the students.

- Plan a popcorn and movie night with all the students.
- If possible, plan an overnight performance trip that ties into a tourist site with strong music connections (theme parks, monuments, or museums).
- Tell your students that you care for them.
- Ask your students questions about their interests.
- Commend your students privately and publicly when you can and when you see exceptional work from them. (You will need to use your own judgment to know whether public or private praise is more appropriate, depending on the situation.)

As you transition into your new job, remember to hold the building of strong relationships with students as a high priority. Understand that one of the main reasons your students will trust you as their leader and strive for excellence is because you have not only demonstrated excellence in your own walk but have also nurtured a professional and caring relationship with them over time.

1. **What is the current social/community health of your music program?**

   _____

2. **In what ways do you think there is room for improvement?**

   _____

3. **What are some practical ways to build community that you are willing to try?**

   _____

Student-to-Student Mentorship

It is also important to try to build and invest in the community outside the four walls of the music room as much as you do inside the music room. A great tool to spur this on is a music mentorship program. In my own practice, I call this mentorship program "Orchestra Buddies," but any name that suits your school can work. Under adult supervision, high school students meet with beginners in my room after school for an hour and go through rhythms, fingerings, techniques, and other topics of music performance on all their class music.

Having older students mentor younger players as a part of their community service hours requirement is a great way to invest in the community and build a strong culture of music even in the younger grades. Throughout this mentorship program, it was also interesting to learn from parents just how much the younger students looked up to their older Orchestra Buddies. They found it to be very cool that they were friends with older students who shared their same passion for music. Watching and listening to older and more advanced players helped them paint a vivid picture in their minds of what they would be capable of in the near future. This was very exciting to them. This type of program was not only a way to build connections within the music program and community but also a way to retain current students for years to come.

This might be more difficult if your school doesn't have multiple levels on campus. If this is the case, and if you haven't done so already, reach out to the directors around your area to see if it is possible to set up a mentoring program. A mentoring program does not have to look exactly like the examples above. It may suit your program better to have students of the same age group mentor each other. You might consider organizing a mentoring program set up for students of the same age but on secondary instruments. It can be organized any way that you see fit to most effectively build relationships and performance success for all your students.

Community Service Performances

Community service performances can have a great effect on your students. Having students reach beyond themselves to serve and brighten the days of others can be a very humbling and gratifying experience for them. Community service performances will also provide your students with a deeper sense of investment in the program. They can begin to focus less on how they can simply perform better than their peers and more on how they can better serve others with their talents.

During my last transition, I learned of a great tradition that had been established in the orchestra program many years before. High school students joined together after school hours to form an ensemble called the Heart Strings Orchestra. This student-led group was responsible for organizing performances for nursing homes and any other venue near the school that would spread cheer through music. It is important to note that all the community service events that you put together will inadvertently double as publicity for your program and as a recruiting tool. This shouldn't be the main focus, but it is nonetheless a real by-product of public performance.

Whether their act of service is performing in a nursing home, playing for and mentoring younger students in their community, playing carols around the holidays, performing valentine-grams, or volunteering for other service-oriented opportunities, find something that will make students think beyond themselves. This shift in focus will provide an added layer of authenticity and humility to their overall experience in your music program.

Establishing a Rapport with the Athletic Department

Establishing a rapport with your athletic department will be an important task as you transition into your new school. It will be good for you to understand any standing policies for schedule conflicts between athletic games and important performances and field trips. How often do these conflicts happen, if at all? How will these issues be resolved? Is there a written policy? Take the time to introduce yourself to the department and put names and faces together. It may be harder to dismiss the needs of your program when it comes to situations like these if a personal relationship (even if it is superficial) is established.

Establishing a Rapport with the Maintenance Department

As you settle into your new position, be sure to build a rapport with the maintenance staff (even if it is superficial) as well. Say hi and get to know their names. There will undoubtedly come a time when you need an emergency favor that involves heavy lifting or some kind of repair. The maintenance staff may be much more inclined to help you without having to go through all the paperwork if they know you and have had conversations with you. Be sure not to abuse this relationship and only call in a favor if it is an absolute emergency.

Student Leadership

If possible, have your new students take on leadership roles. Get them involved and delegate responsibilities. This can be anything from organizing music to serving as social chair, leading warmups, or being section leaders. The students' investment in the program will help solidify their ownership and the authenticity of the entire experience.

Closing Letter and Play on Words

At the risk of being completely cringeworthy, I want to share a fun gimmick that I use to bring each school year to a close. At the end of each year, I write a thank-you letter to all the students in the program, and I somehow weave every repertoire selection title from that year into it. This is a great way to make the students laugh, but it also brings all their accomplishments into focus and on paper. Here is a sample of the last letter I wrote to my students at the end of a school year before my transition:

> Dear Orchestra Students,
>
> What a *"Boisterous Bourree"* of a year! Like *"Clock Work,"* another year has passed. Let me start by saying that you all are the reason I do what I do. Working with you all is one of *"My Favorite Things"* in the world! As you know, I am at a *"Turning Point"* in my life, and so are you. I am moving on to work in a new school next year, and many of you are faced with the decision of whether or not to continue with your music education. My hope for all of you is that you do continue. This is your *"Simple Gift"* or your *"Little Symphony,"* meant for you to enjoy for the rest of your lives through the good times and *"In the Bleak Midwinters."* I'm not saying it's always going to be a *"Cakewalk,"* but do it with *"Bells and Buccaneers"* and a smile! You have developed so much *"Momentum"* on your instruments, and I would hate to see all of that come to a *"Finale."* This year is just the musical *"Prelude"* of greater things to come. Your music has the potential to open a whole *"Winter Milky Way"* of opportunities. Keep going!

I am so proud of all of you. You have been on a *"Majestic March"* of *"A Hero's Journey"* and back. At the *"Western Dawn"* of this year, I never would have imagined that you all would have accomplished all that you have. All of you have exceeded my expectations! I know I ask a lot of you all, and there are a lot of things in your lives to juggle as though it were some kind of *"Tango d'Amour,"* but I am so impressed with the way you guys handle it with grace and perseverance. Thank you for trusting me. ☺ Keep working hard! Practice, practice, practice! I will always be here for you, and I'm just a click away. I love you all! All the best.

Sincerely,
Mr. Gordon

This tool definitely is not for every teacher and every program. You may find other ways to bring about community and laughter. Whatever you can do to bring your students closer together and invest more in their music education, do it.

Recruiting

Recruiting is a critical part of developing and maintaining a strong music program. Without recruiting, your program will be unsustainable. Doing nothing to bring new students in is not an option. Students leave programs, whether it's by way of dropping out, moving to different schools, or graduating out. Therefore, it is essential to continually recruit so that you have a steady influx of students from year to year.

You may be coming into a position that is new and never had a set recruiting practice. You also may be coming into a program that is on the smaller side and that you would like to see grow in numbers, or you may be coming into a very well-established program that has a well-organized system of recruiting. With the last scenario in particular, the trick is to maintain what has been working. As discussed in chapter 6, don't make unnecessary alterations or institute change for the sake of change. Sometimes, standing still *is* moving forward.

As music educators, we have the opportunity to recruit in several different ways. We can recruit by sparking interest in the untapped talent within the current student body, serving the community in and out of school through music performances, and developing relationships with feeder programs.

♫ Recruiting from the Current Student Body

Within the current student body, there is untapped talent that may be delighted to experience the fun of being in an ensemble. Here are some practical ideas:

Bring a Friend to Music Day

Talk to your students ahead of time and ask them to bring a friend who is musical but is not putting their talent to use in the school. Make this a fun, interactive event (snacks are always great) that they can participate in through dialogue, questions, and touching the instruments. This is an opportunity for you to show them what they are missing out on, so make it fun! (This would be an in-house field trip, which needs to be approved by your supervisor or principal.)

Public Performances

As you begin to get the ball rolling with developing your program, good publicity is key. Play at school assemblies and events so that the rest of the student body can hear great instruments and music performed by their peers. Play as often as you can and as well as you can. If public performances are difficult to organize, consider taking high-quality, short video clips of your group or groups rehearsing to share on the school social media page if possible. Remember, good publicity is key when it comes to recruiting!

1. **If feasible, how do you plan to promote and recruit from the current student body?**

   _____

2. **Who do you need to talk to in order to get this started?**

   _____

3. **What are some alternative ideas that you have in mind to recruit from the current student body?**

   _____

♬ Recruiting from Feeder Programs

It is important to try to develop a relationship with your feeder programs. Here are some practical ideas:

- Perform for your feeder programs and have a Q&A session.
- Write a letter to the parents currently in your program before elective-selection season and ask them to be ambassadors for your program to any prospective families that they know. Sometimes, word-of-mouth promotion from a happy family can be the best recruiting tool.
- Create a short video introducing yourself and the music program. This video can include good characteristic performance samples of each individual instrument as well as a sample of your large ensemble. This video concept can be very useful, especially if you are trying to connect with prospective families moving to your community from out

of the city or out of state.

- Write a letter to the prospective parents and ask your feeder program colleagues to forward it. This should be a letter that gives prospective parents a little information about your program and the benefits of music in general. Let them know that you are available to help and answer any questions. Developing a relationship with those families early on can make a big difference.
- Have an instrument petting zoo family event. An instrument petting zoo is an educational tool that allows parents and students to see and manipulate the instruments in person.

1. **Who do you need to talk to in order to get started with recruiting from your feeder programs?**

_____

2. **What tools do you plan to use in order to recruit?**

_____

♫ Sharing Your Students' Accomplishments

As you carry on about your days in your new position, it is easy to lose sight of all the current student stories. It is extremely important to keep building your new community by sharing the success stories of your students with the entire school. Knowing the students' accomplishments gives everyone the opportunity to be more invested in their future work and success. If you have had a less-than-easy time gelling with your new community, it is harder for people who are on the fence about your new leadership to argue with the success of the students.

Make sure to publicize your students' success stories as much as possible. Email and social media are the easiest tools to speak directly to large groups of people at the same time. (Check with your administration for social media posting guidelines.) Here are some ideas of success stories to share with everyone in your school:

- The day after a successful performance, send a congratulatory email to students and parents. (Copy your administrators on this email, and add pictures if possible.) Make sure the email is positive and to the point.

    Dear *[Orchestra/Band/Choir]* Families,

    I would like to formally congratulate you and your children for a wonderful concert last night. The students were amazing! They were so enthusiastic and professional in their presentation. I loved their energy! What a great way to kick off the *[HOLIDAYS, SPRING, OR SUMMER SEASON]*. I was so very proud of the students. I ask a lot of them, but they are all developing into fine musicians. I have seen so much growth in all of them since the beginning of this school year. They possess so much promise and potential, and I am so happy to see them tapping into it! Thank you for supporting your child's music education and the *[SCHOOL]* Music Department. This is truly a special place! I enjoy working with your children so much, and I consider it an honor to be their director. I am excited to see what the future has in store for them on their musical journey. The sky's the limit! :)

    Sincerely,
    Mr./Mrs./Ms. *[YOUR NAME]*

- Send a school-wide email that lists the district or state evaluation results of your students' solos, festivals, or statewide auditions. If your students scored particularly well at an evaluation, send the judges' score sheets so people can better understand the categories and demands of the discipline.

- If your school has a weekly, biweekly, or monthly parent newsletter, include your students' accomplishments in that letter.
- Post results of district and state evaluations on social media with pictures.
- Post short video excerpts of well-rehearsed music that sounds great on social media to get people interested in what you are doing in the classroom and excited to come hear the students perform live.
- Email and post pictures of community service events or performances.
- Email and post pictures of fun community- or team-building events (movie nights, bowling, kickball, or music field trips).
- Send a school-wide email listing students who have auditioned and been selected for county, state, or national honor performance groups.
- Publicly recognize and celebrate the accomplishments of your students at your concerts, where you have a captive audience. Highlight performance evaluation results, county, state, and national honor ensemble participation, and community service projects completed by the students.

1. **What are some accomplishments of your students that you can immediately share with your school community?**

_____

_____

2. **What medium will you be using to share the accomplishments of your students?**

_____

_____

CHAPTER 8

"The Other Side" by SZA & Justin Timberlake

Oh No! The Grass Isn't Greener!

When you decide to take the plunge and move from one position to the next, it is most likely because the new position being presented to you is alluring and holds the promise of being better. The new position appears to be a step up, and in some ways it probably is. But what happens when, unbeknownst to you, in some very specific and important ways, it's *not* better?

Many people, including myself, have experienced this phenomenon. In my previous transition, I was very excited to take over the program. I was eager to work very hard to win the hearts of the students. One of the hopes that I had going into the position was that everyone would love making music as much as I did. I imagined that everyone would welcome what I perceived to be positive changes. I also thought the school culture would appreciate the arts as much as my previous school did. All these things were reasonable expectations.

The difficulty that I had was dealing with the realization that none of these things were exactly as I had imagined and that my expectations would not come to fruition for several years. This was a shock to my system and may be a shock to yours if you find yourself in a similar situation.

First, know that you are not alone. Many people feel the same way when they are stepping into new positions with hidden land mines. It is normal for people to sometimes go through the emotions of buyer's remorse when making major career changes. This doesn't make you foolish, gullible, or weak. On the contrary, this makes you human! Some negative and undesired circumstances will simply be unknown to you until you've already immersed yourself in your new position. Don't beat yourself up, and don't let it get to you. Think positively and start cultivating a solution-oriented mindset.

Don't freak out!

One of the quirky phrases that I always have written up on my whiteboard for students to see is "Rule 1: 'Don't freak out.' " I started using this phrase during my last transition to a new school. With the changes that I was bringing about, students seemed to panic and lose sight of the main goals of the class: having fun through learning and developing a profound appreciation for music. Some of the changes that I was making to the program brought about anxiety for some parents and students, which ultimately led to some of them quitting altogether. I tried my best to reassure them that sometimes it's best to just breathe and not "freak out."

From experience, I know that if they had taken a moment to breathe and talk things through ("Don't freak out!"), those students would have realized that staying in the program was the most beneficial thing for them. With calmness comes perspective and clarity of mind. This line of thinking ended up helping most of my students transition from the old way of doing things to the new way of doing things. But I digress.

Now to turn a corner and bring it back to the grass not being greener, is the job not really what you expected? Were people not as friendly as you had been led to believe? Were you presented a completely different picture of what you would be getting into? Whatever the situation may be, remember this phrase: "Don't freak out!" Give yourself time to breathe and evaluate. Remember, with calmness comes perspective and clarity of mind. Do a cost-benefit analysis of your current position, and ask yourself some of these questions:

1. What are the things within your power that you can improve?
2. What are some of the troubling things that will never change, no matter how hard you try? Can you live with them?
3. Are you being reasonable?
4. Are you being flexible?
5. How can you adapt to your new setting so that you can reach your personal best?
6. What are the positives about the new position that are exciting? Do these outweigh the negatives?
7. Is there an opportunity for a dialogue with someone higher up to express concerns and discuss how to possibly bring about positive changes?
8. What specifically are deal-breakers for you?

After asking yourself these important questions, there are a few tips you can keep in the back of your mind to help you stay level-headed as you go through your transition.

♫ **Create a plan.**

Create a plan for systematically addressing your concerns. Some of your concerns may be within your power to change, and some may not. Journaling may help you sort through your thoughts so that you can better address your concerns. Set attainable goals and a reasonable timeline for the change you would like to see to be personally satisfied, and remain motivated.

♫ Give it time.

This may seem cliché, but sometimes all you need is patience in the midst of a storm if you want to make it to dry, sunny weather. In my experience, I have seen that the development of a new or transitioning program with a new director takes about three to five years to settle in. That means patience is key. Sometimes time, distance, and perspective are necessary elements to truly appreciate the progress you are making in a challenging situation. Put your patience to the test and give it time to improve.

♫ Look forward, not backward.

The disappointment of plans not working out as you had hoped can be very discouraging and can make you long for what you once had. We can never go back to a particular moment in time and relive it. At best, we can try to recreate it, but it will never be that actual moment. If the grass isn't greener in your new position, it is okay to lament what was lost. The greener grass may have turned out to be a shade darker than expected, but the key is to not dwell on what was lost and to *keep moving forward to the next positive pathway*. Plant new seeds and keep searching for the brightest shade of green around you.

♫ Changing Faces

Something to also remember as you navigate through difficult changes is that change itself is constant. The parents and students who are not receptive to you and your procedures will eventually move on. Kids graduate, change schools, and pick other electives. Colleagues leave, and administrators retire. Change keeps happening. Now, I wouldn't bank on the possibility of people leaving as your sole coping mechanism for difficult work situations, but it's just something to remember when your purpose and passion seem distant. Keep your standard of excellence high and don't waver. Remember that no school or music program is perfect. There will never be the perfect situation, only the situations that you strive to make better.

♫ Keep your résumé updated.

At times, you may feel discouraged with the progress you are making in your new position. If things seem bleak, update your résumé. Keeping your résumé updated in a less-than-ideal work environment can have a few positive outcomes. The most obvious outcome would be that it keeps you ready to take advantage of any unforeseen opportunities that may come your way at any given time. If you do eventually decide (after very careful consideration) to look for a new position, you have kept yourself market-ready.

Another outcome of keeping your résumé updated is that it serves as an emotional reminder that you have a lot to offer the profession of music education. Updating your résumé forces you to reflect on your body of work and your past accomplishments. Sometimes, seeing your achievements on paper makes them feel more tangible.

Updating and reviewing your accomplishments may also help to rebuild some lost confidence due to a challenging work environment. This doesn't need to turn into a self-adulation session, but rather, it can be something more productive and useful. Let it serve as a reminder that your current circumstances, if not ideal, are not necessarily representative of your entire career. You are a wonderful and capable professional, and now you have the résumé to prove it. Take even your small accomplishments as victories and write them down. Even if you only have one thing you can update, make sure you do it.

♫ Don't be afraid to look elsewhere.

- *"When your soul leaves the job, take your body with it."* —Unknown
- *"There's a difference between quitting and knowing when you've had enough."* —Unknown

If all else fails and your current work situation does not improve and seems unsustainable, don't be afraid or ashamed to look elsewhere. Not every position will be a great fit, and that's okay. Incongruence is a natural part of life, and your work environment is not exempt from that reality. Do your best to be positive and to learn as much as you can from where you are before you move on. It is important that you are in a positive working environment where you feel respected, secure, and productive. If the environment you are in is irredeemably toxic, then the best thing for your physical, emotional, and mental health is to find a new position— the question is, *Where* are you best suited to offer the best parts of yourself?

♫ Interview Questions for the Future

There will never be a perfect school or music program, but sometimes the questions that we ask during interviews can help us discover the level of compatibility that we have with a particular school and music program. This is not to say that if you ask all the right questions, everything will be perfect, but rather, the idea is to ask the right questions to help prevent you from ending up in a similar situation. Remember, this interview is just as much for you to gauge your compatibility with the prospective school as it is for the school to gauge their compatibility with you. Here are some questions to consider asking during your next interview:

- Why is this position open?
- What are the average class sizes in the program?
- How would you describe the level of academic engage-

ment of the students in the school?

- What would you like to see from a new hire in the first year?
- What is your vision for this music program in the next three to five years?
- In what ways does this school support the arts?
- What is the music culture like at this school? Can you share how I might experience that in the role that I am applying for?
- What are the aligning standards and expectations across band, choir, and orchestra?
- What are some of the challenges the previous music director had in this position?
- What is your biggest concern about this program?
- How are performance and success measured in this particular position?
- What does excellence look like to you with regard to this music program?
- How would you describe your leadership style?
- What is the school policy or practice for teachers wanting to pursue higher education, professional development coursework, clinics, and conventions?
- What are your music facilities like?
- What does a typical day for someone in this position look like?
- What protocols are in place to ensure the performing arts and athletic departments can work in harmony?
- What is the music budget?

1. **Is the grass greener in your new position? If so, in what ways?**

_____

_____

2.   If the grass isn't greener, what have you learned?

_____

_____

3.   Looking back to your interview, what important questions
     could you have asked your hiring committee to help you
     make a more informed decision?

_____

_____

4.   Are there any legitimate concerns that you can address that
     may be causing students to feel discouraged and leave? If
     so, what are they, and how do you intend to address them?

_____

_____

CHAPTER 9

*"The Greatest Show" performed by Hugh Jackman,
Keala Settle, Zac Efron & Zendaya*

Letting Your Concert Embody Your Vision of Excellence

C oncerts are a pivotal part of the discipline of music. Whether a concert is formal or informal, knowing that they will be performing for an audience can give students a tangible reason to aspire to reach their personal best. It also gives them a chance to shine in front of their community and showcase their accomplishments from one season of learning to the next.

A successful concert has the potential to recruit students, parents, and administrators to your cause. I have personally seen students and parents who were on the fence about remaining in music decide to stick with it after experiencing a great concert. The stage, the lights, the audience, and the excitement all can really help motivate students to push forward with their music education.

After my first concert in my last job transition, one of my colleagues reported back to me that they overheard parents in the audience saying, "Now I see why he makes them work so hard; this is the best I've ever heard them sound." That concert was a turning point for me in getting people to understand my philosophy and approach to participating in an instrumental music program. My methodology may have been different from that of my predecessor, but that didn't make it any less legitimate or effective.

So, what does a successful concert look like? In my opinion, it looks like students dressed appropriately and looking uniform, sounding good, demonstrating focus and discipline for their craft, and, most importantly, having a clear display of fun through the learning process. Though your general audience member may not be able to articulate what specifically makes a great concert, you can, and the elements listed above are a great starting point.

You may have a few ideas of your own that speak to what a great concert should look like. Tailor all these elements to fit the specifics of your program and make your concerts as memorable as possible.

Invite your feeder program.

A great way to help increase interest and possibly bring new students into the ranks is to invite your feeder program to your concerts. If your concert is well planned and fun, younger students will be excited and motivated to join. You can even do a group acknowledgment (ask the students from that feeder school to stand so they can be applauded) to make those students feel special. Publicly let them know that you are thankful for their attendance and that you look forward to working with them in the near future. If you want to take things a step further, you can even coordinate with the younger students' current directors to see if there is an easier piece that all the students can perform together to promote community and belonging.

This is an opportunity to promote buy-in not only with your current community but with your future pupils as well.

♫ A Captive Audience

Concerts can also be a great transitioning tool for you to formally introduce yourself to the community and share your vision. A concert, by definition, is a captive audience that is ready to listen. You have the floor! Being the emcee of the concert, you literally have the microphone and can gracefully drop truth nuggets on your audience.

These truth nuggets can be things that the audience may not have ever thought about or heard before. While you don't want to take away from the actual performance of your students by talking too much, you can most certainly find a way to weave in some of the positive ideas, fun classroom and rehearsal experiences, accomplishments, and events to look forward to that pertain to your program.

Here are some ideas you can very quickly weave throughout your talks on the microphone:

- You can mention music education advocacy and research that supports the arts and undergirds the rationale behind your students electing to take music. (Be very brief and don't go overboard.)
- You can mention challenges your students have overcome. (Everyone loves a success story.)
- You can mention some of the unique techniques that the audience will be hearing from the students on their instruments.
- You can briefly mention the background of the composer whose music is being performed and their intent behind the piece.
- You can even keep things lighthearted and mention some fun and quirky classroom experiences between yourself and the students preparing for the concert.
- You can mention student accolades and achievements.

- You can mention praiseworthy and thoughtful comments or actions by students from throughout the semester.
- You can publicly thank those who have been allies to you and your students, such as administrators, faculty, private teachers, maintenance employees, or donors.

The reality is, the floor is yours to say what you want (positive comments only and within reason) to help bolster goodwill, buy-in, and commitment to the program. Please remember that the audience is primarily there to hear music, not a lecture, so whatever you want or need to say should be short, sweet, and to the point.

It would be wise to write down the specific things you want to say and when you want to say them. Rehearse them ahead of time so that you have an easier time reciting them when you are on stage. Whatever you choose to talk about, remember that it is an opportunity for your vision of community, dedication, and excellence to be on full display.

♫ Quality vs. Quantity

Many educators would argue that getting students performing is an essential part of building a strong, fun, and exciting program. In many cases, setting up performance opportunities lends itself to students practicing more and, hence, being more invested in their own musical growth—but I would add a disclaimer to that idea: make sure that you are able to balance your performances so that the *quality* of each performance is prioritized just as much as the *quantity* of performances.

The excitement of getting ensembles performing can occasionally overshadow the need to make sure students are performing to the best of their ability. Don't over-program performances (playing music that is too hard), especially if the students only have a short window to prepare. Don't be afraid to perform easier, more attainable, and more accessible music that allows the students to sound great and feel good about their work. Audiences are generally unaware of the grade level of music they're hearing. They will, however, be acutely aware if the music they are listening to is out of tune or out of rhythm. So remember, quality and quantity should go hand in hand.

♫ Practical Performance Tips

Here are some practical performance tips that you may want to consider before your next concert. This is not an exhaustive list, but it will help you think through your concert setup with a more critical eye so that, at the end of the day, you are showcasing your and your students' best work.

- Have fun and incorporate appropriate humor.
- Briefly mention the highlights of your time with the students on stage.
- Don't over-program a concert with music that is too hard.
- Choose varied repertoire.
- Be mindful of how long your concert will be. Leave the audience wanting more. Try not to make your concert too long. Map out the expected time it will take to complete the concert.
- If possible, do a dress rehearsal in the performance space.
- Have students help with moving chairs, stands, and other equipment. Give them specific tasks to complete so they have more skin in the game than just performing.
- Write down the specific things you want to say, and rehearse them so that you have an easier time reciting them when you are on stage.
- If possible, run your rehearsals like a performance every day for a week before your concert with great attention to detail in everything that you do.
- Review concert etiquette with your students. Reviewing these concepts will give your students a clear vision of

what is expected of them at any given moment, whether they are on stage performing or not. Here are some practices you can go over to help make the concert enjoyable for yourself and others:

- stage entrances and exits
- tuning sequences
- managing performance mistakes
- transitions, if there are multiple ensembles performing
- when to bow, if applicable
- attentiveness to the conductor
- when to clap

- Have a run sheet or program-order sheet made only for students (different from a program booklet) that lays out what all of your ensembles will be playing and doing at any given time during the concert. This run sheet will inform all of your students of what is to come, even when they are not playing.

- Have your students wear formal uniform attire. Whether it is school-issued concert attire, all black, or black and white, make sure it is all uniform and formal. I have found that the more formally a student dresses, the more committed they are to acting in accordance with the way they are dressed.

Have a list ready of people you want to thank who deserve your public praise.

♫ Program Booklets

In my experience, program booklets tend to be keepsakes for friends and families. Providing a stellar program booklet can help leave a good impression of your leadership with your new community. Every school will have different budgetary constraints. Pick and choose a few enhancements to your program booklet (or even one!), according to your budget and personal tastes. Here are some examples:

- Consider having a themed concert to help bring the whole musical experience together. This can be fun not only for your students but for your audience as well.

- Include a special picture of your graduating students in the program booklet. This can be a dangling carrot for rising students in the program.

- If you don't have the space or finances to create a more extensive program booklet, add in a QR code that leads to a slideshow of your students. Be sure to take lots of pictures throughout the school year. Parents love to see candid photos of their children having fun and learning in their school environment.

- Include a call to action in the program booklet that encourages audience members to post their wonderful photos of the concert on social media and use hashtags associated with your school or district.

- Write a short and positive director's note to go in the program. Explain your vision for the evening. Talk about the pride you have in your students and share a personal anecdote about your experience putting the concert together. This will give your community an opportunity to get to know you better.

- Have a colleague edit the program booklet to minimize the possibility of mistakes making it into the final printing.

Program booklets will not solely make or break the quality of a concert, but they do have the capacity to enhance it. Decide what type of program works best for your concert. The nicer the program is, the more it will complement the wonderful playing of your students.

♬ Concert Logistics

Having a checklist can help you organize your concert logistics so that the concert runs as smoothly as possible. Here is a checklist template that can be adjusted to fit your particular needs:

CONCERT CHECKLIST

ONE MONTH PRIOR:	TWO WEEKS PRIOR:
☐ Email parents concert details (date, time, place, dress code)	☐ Release the concert trailer to school community
☐ Contact teacher volunteers if necessary	☐ Send reminder email to parents and students about upcoming concert (date, time, place, dress code)
☐ Contact parent volunteers	☐ Create slide shows or videos to be displayed at the concert
☐ Start creating a concert trailer	☐ Design program booklet
☐ Check with maintenance and IT department for any concert needs	

ONE WEEK PRIOR:	SHOW DAY:
☐ Invite a colleague to classes for constructive critiques	☐ Send reminder email to parents and students
☐ Proof the program booklet (names, grades, spelling, etc.) and get it printed	☐ Direct parent volunteers to decorate and block off reserved seating
☐ Create concert speech, student awards, and concert run sheet	☐ Organize music scores for concert
☐ Assign volunteers their specific tasks	☐ Review concert speech and student awards
☐ Dress rehearsal	☐ Proofread speech

FOR MUSICIANS (ONE WEEK PRIOR):
☐ Reiterate the importance of daily practice
☐ Try on performance uniform to make sure everything fits properly
☐ Organize all sheet music in concert order
☐ Review concert etiquette
☐ Review concert arrival (seating, case storage, etc.) and departure (cleanup) expectations

As you go through your transition, remember that your concerts are a great tool to help people get to know you and buy into your vision. Watching the students achieve excellence in real time is a great way to win over the skeptics who haven't quite bought into your leadership style. Take the time to carefully plan out all the details of your concert to make it as smooth, fun, and enjoyable as possible.

1. What are some ideas from this chapter that you can incorporate into your concerts to help demonstrate your vision for the program?

_____

_____

2. Realistically, how many performances do you think your ensembles are capable of this year, given your school schedule and your students' level of playing?

_____

_____

3. What specifically will you do to help enhance those performances to make each one feel unique and special?

_____

_____

4. What are some practical concert tips from this chapter that would be easy to implement and would make your concert logistics run smoother?

_____

_____

5. What are some practical concert tips of your own that were not in this chapter and that you would like to include in

your own program?

_____

_____

CHAPTER 10

"At Last" by Etta James

Making Your Vision Come to Fruition

T he last chapter of your transition can only truly be written by you. This is your story. The final outcome will look different for everyone, depending on circumstances, experiences, backgrounds, and preferences.

Think back to what made you fall in love with music in the first place. What inspired you to become the educated professional you are today? Reflect on ways to emulate that experience with your own students. Remember, you didn't get to where you are in your new position on a whim or by being a slouch. You had to take action and make things happen. You are good at what you do, and you will only continue to grow wiser in your professional life.

In the next few pages, you will find the skeleton of an All Things Considered action plan to help you focus and clarify your ideas as you transition into your new position. All things should be given consideration, including giving yourself grace as you move into a new professional chapter in life. Take the time to go through all the questions, and review all your reflective responses that you wrote throughout the previous chapters as well. There is also a transitioning teacher music playlist to help you stay on track musically and emotionally. Leave it, add to it, or take away from it, whichever suits your preferences. The hope is that it can bring you some relaxation.

Evaluate and document your progress throughout the school year in the Progress Reflection sections at the end of this chapter. This will help you to see the bigger picture and what direction you need to go in the next few years of your transition. Once you have successfully completed your transition, pay it forward. Be ready and willing to share your experiences, methods, and ideas with others.

Final Note to Self: Remember to always work hard, stay positive, be kind, be creative, be organized, be methodical, have fun, and, most importantly, take care of yourself physically, mentally, and emotionally!

Transitioning Teachers' Playlist

- "Human Nature" Michael Jackson
- "There Will Never Be Another You" Chet Baker
- "Takin' Care of Business" Bachman-Turner Overdrive
- "We Are Family" Sister Sledge
- "It's So Hard to Say Goodbye to Yesterday" Boyz II Men
- "Signed, Sealed, Delivered (I'm Yours)" Stevie Wonder
- "Change the World" Eric Clapton
- "Waterfalls" TLC
- "Happy Together" The Turtles
- "The Other Side" SZA & Justin Timberlake
- "The Greatest Show" Hugh Jackman, Keala Settle, Zac Efron & Zendaya
- "At Last" Etta James

- Bonus Track: "I Have Confidence" from *The Sound of Music*
- Bonus Track: "The Remedy (I Won't Worry)" by Jason Mraz
- Bonus Track: "Waterfalls" by TLC
- Bonus Track: "Waiting on the World to Change" by John Mayer

All Things Considered Action Plan

1. **What attracted you to this new position? Remember this if/ when you feel discouraged.**

   _____

2. **What is the school's vision for your program? Have they communicated this to you?**

   _____

3. **What are you most excited about in your new position?**

   _____

4. **What are you most nervous about as you go into your new position?**

   _____

5. **What are you most confident about with regard to your new position?**

   _____

6. **What personal boundaries are you willing to set to protect your time, as well as your mental and emotional health?**

_____

7. What are your plans to cope with stress?

_____

8. Who are you? (3–5 positive and descriptive words)

_____

9. What is the date on which you will meet and talk with the outgoing director, if possible?

_____

10. What questions do you need answered about your new school?

_____

11. Who do you plan to have as a mentor during your first year of transition?

_____

12. Write out your after-summer routine or to-do list.

_____

13. What is your plan to connect with the students to show them that you care?

_____

14. What is your vision statement for you and your students to

always refer back to?

_____

15. **What does your vision of success look like? Can you articulate it?**

_____

16. **Do you have a model of your vision of success?**

_____

17. **What are the current performance levels of the program?**

_____

18. **What are some curriculum ideas that you intend to bring into your new program?**

_____

19. **What are some specific goals you have for the program?**

_____

20. **Have a conversation and ask your new students to list their music goals for the year. Write down 3–5 goals that stand out to you.**

_____

21. **What commonalities do you see between your goals and the students' goals?**

22. **What are some roadblocks you foresee encountering during your transition?**

23. What are some creative solutions you have come up with to circumvent your possible roadblocks?

Repertoire Ideas

1. _____

2. _____

3. _____

4. _____

5. _____

Field Trip Ideas

Year 1 Priority

Describe your method of implementation.

_____

_____

Year 2 Priority

_____

_____

Describe your method of implementation.

_____

_____

Year 3 Priority

_____

_____

Describe your method of implementation.

_____

_____

One-Month Progress Reflection

_____

_____

_____

_____

_____

_____

_____

_____

_____

_____

_____

_____

_____

_____

_____

_____

_____

_____

_____

_____

_____

_____

_____

Three-Month Progress Reflection

Six-Month Progress Reflection

_____

_____

_____

_____

_____

_____

_____

_____

_____

_____

_____

_____

_____

_____

_____

_____

_____

_____

_____

_____

_____

_____

Eight-Month Progress Reflection

Year-End Reflection

- What ideas did you implement this school year that you would like to see continue?
- What ideas did you implement this school year that you want to tweak and improve?
- What ideas did you implement this school year that you would like to do away with?
- What was the most enjoyable part of the year?
- Where were your students most successful this year?

_____

_____

_____

_____

_____

_____

_____

_____

_____

_____

_____

_____

_____

_____

_____

About the Author

Adrian Gordon is an internationally performed composer and seasoned music educator born and raised in Miami, Florida. After 17 years of teaching music in the classroom in South Florida and going through four music director job transitions in two different schools, as well as general music, choir, and two string orchestra positions, Adrian felt as though there was a gap in his music education training. Even though his undergraduate (BA music) and graduate programs (MS music education) were musically and pedagogically extensive, he never felt as though they touched on those hard-to-navigate areas of transitioning between jobs.

He began writing his debut book after obsessing over his own transitions and trying to manage change and expectations. Adrian believes in the power of music education in a child's life and understands the necessity of having passionate, confident, and supported music teachers at the helm, promoting great musical experiences for students.

When he's not in the classroom, Adrian enjoys composing music and spending time with his wife, Kelly, and their two sons.

Acknowledgments

My greatest debt of gratitude is to my Lord and Savior, Jesus Christ. Thank you, Lord, for all that I am and for all that you continue to do in my life. I am forever grateful and in awe of your love and mercy that you have bestowed upon my life.

I want to thank my awesome wife, Kelly, for all she does, from helping with book edits and all my music career decisions, to putting together my makeshift office so I could tinker in our garage like a musical mad scientist. I couldn't have written this book without you. Thank you, my darling. I love you!

Thank you to my parents, Ray and Joy Gordon, for always believing in me, encouraging me, and supporting me. I could not ask for better parents or for a better upbringing. I still want to be like you both when I grow up. You are my heroes. I love you guys!

Thank you to my brothers, Andre Gordon and Adam Gordon, for always finding the fun, cinematic moments in life to make me laugh. Our brotherly bond has helped me through many a hard time and is life-giving to my soul.

Thank you to my best friend, musical mastermind Ron Castonguay. I don't think I could have gotten through the writing process without your constant encouragement and heart-to-heart conversations. Your friendship has been invaluable to me. Thank you for keeping me grounded but, at the same time, helping me to fly.